THE BIBLE AND THE LAND

THE BIBLE
AND THE LAND

UNCOVER THE ANCIENT CULTURE, DISCOVER HIDDEN MEANINGS

GARY M. BURGE

ZONDERVAN®

ZONDERVAN.com/
AUTHOR**TRACKER**
follow your favorite authors

ZONDERVAN

The Bible and the Land
Copyright © 2009 by Gary M. Burge

Requests for information should be addressed to:

Zondervan, *Grand Rapids, Michigan 49530*

Library of Congress Cataloging-in-Publication Data

Burge, Gary M.
      The Bible and the land / Gary M. Burge.
         p. cm. — (Ancient context, ancient faith)
      ISBN 978-0-310-28044-6 (softcover)
      1. Bible — Geography. 2. Bible — Criticism, interpretation, etc. I. Title.
    BS630.B87 2008
    220.9'1 — dc22   2008026352

Interior design by Kirk DouPonce, www.DogEaredDesign.com
Maps by International Mapping

Printed in China

09 10 11 12 13 14 15 16 17 18 • 15 14 13 12 11 10 9 8 7 6 5 4 3 2 1

For my parents
Who have always brought wisdom
to the wilderness

CONTENTS

SERIES INTRODUCTION   9
Ancient Context, Ancient Faith

1 INTRODUCTION   15
Life, Holy Land, Pilgrimage, and Deserts

2 THE LAND   25

3 WILDERNESS   37
Deuteronomy 6–8; Matthew 4

4 SHEPHERDS   49
Psalm 23; Ezekiel 34; John 10

5 ROCK   61
Deuteronomy 32; Joshua 4; Luke 6:46–49

6 WATER   75
Deuteronomy 11:10; John 4:1–30; 7:37–39

7 BREAD   87
Exodus 16:1–21; John 6:1–58

8 NAMES   99
Exodus 3:13–15; Isaiah 43:1–7; Revelation 3:5

Series Introduction:

ANCIENT CONTEXT, ANCIENT FAITH

EVERY COMMUNITY of Christians throughout history has framed its understanding of spiritual life within the context of its own culture. Byzantine Christians living in the fifth century and Puritan Christians living over a thousand years later used the world in which they lived to work out the principles of Christian faith, life, and identity. The reflex to build house churches, monastic communities, medieval cathedrals, steeple-graced and village-centered churches, or auditoriums with theater seating will always spring from the dominant cultural forces around us.

Even the way we understand "faith in Christ" is to some degree shaped by these cultural forces. For instance, in the last three hundred years, Western Christians have abandoned seeing faith as a chiefly communal exercise (although this is not true in Africa or Asia). Among the many endowments of the European Enlightenment, individualism reigns supreme: Christian faith is a personal, private endeavor. We prefer to say, "*I have accepted Christ,*" rather than define ourselves through a *community* that follows Christ. Likewise (again, thanks to the Enlightenment) we have elevated rationalism as a premier value. Among many Christians faith is a construct of the mind, an effort at knowledge gained through study, an assent to a set of theological propositions. Sometimes even knowing *what you believe* trumps belief itself.

To be sure, many Christians today are challenging these Enlightenment assumptions and are seeking to chart a new path. Nevertheless, this new path is as much a by-product of modern cultural trends than any other. For example, we live today in a highly therapeutic society. Even if we are unaware of the discipline of psychology, we are still being shaped by the values it has brought to our culture over the last hundred years. Faith today has an emotional, feeling-centered basis. Worship is measured by the emotive responses and the heart. "Felt needs" of a congregation shape many sermons.

Therefore, defining Christian faith as a personal choice based on well-informed convictions and inspired by emotionally engaging worship is a formula for spiritual formation that may be natural to us — but it may have elements that are foreign to the experience of other Christians in other cultures or other centuries. I imagine that fifth-century Christians would feel utterly lost in a modern church with its worship band and theater seating where lighting, sound, refreshments, and visual media are closely monitored. They might wonder if this *modern church* was chiefly indebted to entertainment, like a tamed, baptized version of Rome's public arenas. They might also wonder how 10,000 people can gain any sense of shared life or community when each family comes and goes by car, lives a long distance away, and barely recognizes the person sitting next to them.

THE ANCIENT LANDSCAPE

If it is true that *every* culture provides a framework in which the spiritual life is understood, the same must be said about the ancient world. The setting of Jesus and Paul in the Roman Empire was likewise shaped by cultural forces quite different from our own. If we fail to understand these cultural forces, we will fail to understand many of the things Jesus and Paul taught.

This does not mean that the culture of the biblical world enjoys some sort of divine approval or endorsement. We do not need to imitate the biblical world in order to live a more biblical life. This was a culture that had its own preferences for dress, speech, diet, music, intellectual thought, religious expression, and personal identity. And its cultural values were no more significant than are our own. Modesty in antiquity was expressed in a way we may not understand. The arrangement of marriage partners is foreign to our world of personal dating. Even how one prays (seated or standing, arms upraised or folded, aloud or silent) has norms dictated by culture.

But if this is true—if cultural values are presupposed within every faithful community, both now and two thousand years ago—then the stories we read in the Bible may presuppose themes that are completely obscure to us. Moreover, when we read the Bible, we may misrepresent its message because we simply do not understand the cultural instincts of the first century. We live two thousand years distant; we live in the West and the ancient Middle East is not native territory for us.

INTERPRETING FROM AFAR

This means we must be cautious interpreters of the Bible. We must be careful lest we presuppose that *our cultural instincts* are the same as those represented in the Bible. We must be *culturally aware* of our own place in time—and we must work to comprehend the cultural context of the Scriptures that we wish to understand. Too often interpreters have lacked cultural awareness when reading the Scriptures. We have failed to recognize the gulf that exists between who we are today and the context of the Bible. We have forgotten that we read the Bible as foreigners, as visitors who have traveled not only to a new geography but a new century. We are literary tourists who are deeply in need of a guide.

The goal of this series is to be such a guide—to explore themes from the biblical world that are often misunderstood. In what sense, for instance, did the physical geography of Israel shape its people's sense of spirituality? How did the storytelling of Jesus presuppose cultural themes now lost to us? What celebrations did Jesus know intimately (such as a child's birth, a wedding, or a burial)? What agricultural or religious festivals did he attend? How did he use common images of labor or village life or social hierarchy when he taught? Did he use humor or allude to politics? In many cases—just as in our world—the more delicate matters are handled indirectly, and it takes expert guidance to revisit their correct meaning.

In a word, this series employs *cultural anthropology, archaeology, and contextual backgrounds* to open up new vistas for the Christian reader. If the average reader suddenly sees a story or an idea in a new way, if a familiar passage is suddenly opened for new meaning and application, this effort has succeeded.

I am indebted to many experiences and people who awakened my sense of urgency about this interpretive method. My first encounter came as a student at Beirut's *Near East School of Theology* in the 1970s. Since then, scholars such as David Daube, J. D. M. Derrett, S. Safrai, M. Stern, E. P. Sanders, Charles Kraft, James Strange, Kenneth Bailey, Bruce Malina, I. Howard Marshall, and a host of others have contributed to how I read the New Testament. Bailey's many books in particular as well as his long friendship have been prominent in inspiring my efforts into the cultural anthropology of the ancient world. In addition, I have been welcomed many times by the Arabic-speaking church in Lebanon, Syria, Iraq, Jordan, Palestine, and Egypt and there became attuned to the way that cultural setting influences how we read texts. To them and their great and historic faith, I owe a considerable debt.

Finally, special thanks are due to Katya Covrett and Verlyn Verbrugge at Zondervan Publishing. Verlyn's expert editing and Katya's creativity improved the book enormously. Elizabeth Dias, my research assistant, also edited the manuscript and found weaknesses even Verlyn missed. And last (and most important), my wife, Carol, read and critiqued the manuscript during our last sabbatical in Cambridge, England. Her insight and wisdom appear in every chapter.

Soli Deo Gloria.

Gary M. Burge
Wheaton, Illinois

Chapter 1

INTRODUCTION

Life, Holy Land, Pilgrimage, and Deserts

MY LIFE is a life lived alongside the wilderness. Perhaps there was a time (maybe in my early twenties) when I thought that most of life would be akin to a fine day at a southern California beach: low sixties in the morning with a cool, foggy marine layer, bright sun by 11:00 a.m. with good waves forming, palm trees along beachside cliffs, the smell of salt and sand, and no cares other than finding lunch. The perfect burrito no doubt joined to perfect health, outstanding waves, beach music on K-Earth 101, and no cares whatsoever.

To use a biblical metaphor, life was to be all Promised Land and no wilderness, always in Jerusalem without entering the Judean desert.

But it didn't take long for the fantasy to break down. A new picture eventually emerged (maybe in my late twenties), when I began to view life with a very different metaphor: it was Israel's sojourn from Egypt to the Promised Land, a trek out of captivity and through the desert. Even when we arrived at our destination of promise, there were still difficulties with Canaanites and drought and war. And the desert—just east of every city—always remained the same, reminding me of the original pilgrimage and the prospect of going there again.

VIEW OF TEMPLE MOUNT IN JERUSALEM

CAMELS IN THE JUDEAN WILDERNESS

Todd Bolen/www.BiblePlaces.com

It comes as no surprise to me that over the centuries Christians have used the juxtaposition of Promised Land and wilderness as the supreme metaphor for life. On occasion there are moments of genuine wonder, joy, and celebration. On other occasions, there are experiences in the desert wilderness—wildernesses formed through crises of various kinds—and life takes on a confusing, even disturbing, quality.

Ironically, it has been in the wilderness where I've learned most of what I know about God, myself, and the people with whom I live. It was a great discovery when I learned (maybe in my late thirties) that this was a truth held not only by characters throughout the Bible, but by thousands of Christian pilgrims, mystics, and monks who used the wilderness as a metaphor for their own lives—and, in some cases, chose to live in a wilderness (often in Middle Eastern deserts) in order to learn things more deeply.

THE LAND AND PILGRIMAGE

From the beginning, Christians have believed that the land of the Bible held promise for their own spiritual growth, that simply going there and seeing the context of the biblical stories, perhaps recreating experiences known to David or Jesus, might in some way bring renewal or inspiration. This is still true today. Tour buses that cross the Jordan River south of

16   THE BIBLE AND THE LAND

JORDAN RIVER

Galilee almost always make the required stop to baptize travelers who wonder if these waters are different than other waters. They wonder if perhaps being baptized where Jesus was baptized might help them understand their Bible or even give them something they've missed their entire lives.

The first Christian of record to do this was the "Pilgrim of Bordeaux," who came to Jerusalem in about AD 333. His notes circulated widely and by the mid–300s, Christian visitors began arriving in the Holy Land regularly. Travel was dangerous and unforgiving, but the rewards outweighed all dangers.

PORTRAIT OF ST. CYRIL OF JERUSALEM

Besides, a Christian community was there and hospices would extend welcome. The Christian pilgrimage industry had begun. Today two million tourists make the same trip annually.

But this travel was not merely for the sake of curiosity. Fourth-century Christian theologians reflected on the theological meaning of the incarnation (the full entry of God into human life), and this led them to thoughts about the *place* of this incarnation.

CHURCH OF THE HOLY SEPULCHER

St. Cyril was bishop of Jerusalem from 349 to 384 and so had the privilege of presiding over the magnificent new church built above Christ's tomb by the Christian emperor Constantine. He preached a series of sermons just steps from the tomb and there declared the difference of being *in the Holy Land*. "Others only hear, but we both see and touch." For Cyril, the land itself was a living source of witness to our faith (*Catechetical Lectures* 14.23). For him, the land virtually had become a "fifth" gospel.

Jerome (345 – 420), living in Bethlehem, urged the same: "*Here* in Bethlehem he was wrapped in swaddling clothes; *here* he was seen by shepherds, *here* he was pointed out by the star, *here* he was adored by wise men." *This is the beginning of a sacred geography.* Jerome wrote a letter in 386 trying to compel a woman named Marcella to join his pilgrim community in the Holy Land. In it he

A 15TH CENTURY PORTRAIT OF ST. JEROME

describes, perhaps with some exaggeration, the pious flooding to Jerusalem:

> *Every person of note in Gaul hastens here. The Briton, "sundered from our world," no sooner makes progress in religion than he leaves the setting sun in quest of a spot of which he knows only through Scripture and common report. Need we recall the Armenians, the Persians, the peoples of India and Arabia? Or those of our neighbor, Egypt, so rich in monks; of Pontus and Cappadocia; of Syria and Mesopotamia and the teeming east? In fulfillment of the Savior's words, "Wherever the body is, there will the eagles be gathered together," they all assemble here and exhibit in this one city the most varied virtues. Differing in speech, they are one in religion, and almost every nation has a choir of its own. (Letters 46:10).*

Notes about the early pilgrims are few. But we do have one account from the first-known woman pilgrim named Egeria. She lived in the late 300s and came from a town along the European Atlantic coast, perhaps France or Spain. Clearly Egeria was on a quest to understand her Christian faith. And as she moved closer to the Holy Land, her narrative filled with expansive descriptions and hopes for inspiration. She wanted to see holy sites — but more than this, she was eager to learn about the local church, its liturgies, and its history.

She arrived in Jerusalem in 381 and spent three years recording carefully all of the worship liturgies she witnessed

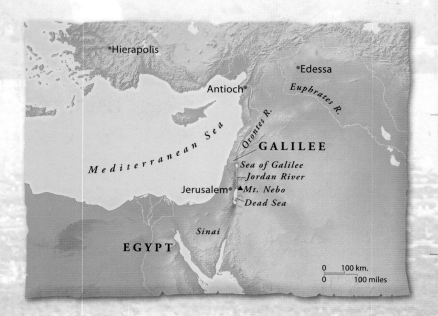

for her "sisters" who lived at home in Europe. She also made numerous trips to Egypt, Sinai, Galilee, even Mount Nebo (where Moses was buried). Then she traveled north, heading for the famous city of Antioch on the Orontes River. From there she went east to ancient Hierapolis ("a city of great plenty, rich and very beautiful," *Egeria's Travels* 18:1), crossing the Euphrates River ("We

St. Catherine's monastery located at the base of Mt. Sinai

had to cross in ships, big ones, and that meant I spent a half day there," 18:2), and came to the ancient city of Edessa (modern Turkish Sanli Urfa). Here the bishop greeted her warmly. Egeria wrote:

> The holy bishop of the city was a truly devout man, both monk and confessor. He welcomed me and said, "My daughter, I can see what a long journey this is on which your faith has brought you — right to the other end of the earth. So now please let us show you all the places Christians should visit here." I gave thanks to God, and eagerly accepted the bishop's invitation. (*Egeria's Travels* 19:5)

What instincts drove Egeria? Why did she think that visiting the Holy Land would be instructive and beneficial? Why did monks begin migrating to this part of the world to build desert communities and cave dwellings within the same century? A visitor to Syria, Egypt, or even the deserts east of Jerusalem can still find the remains of their monasteries. West of Cairo the monasteries of Wadi Natrun are home to a community of six hundred monks.

What does this land have to teach?

THE LAND AND SPIRITUAL PROMISE

Countless pilgrims have followed in Egeria's footsteps every year, coming to the Holy Land in search of some inspiration or understanding that they cannot gain at home. For most Protestants, it is a quest to recover the historical locations of past events. There is a "pilgrim trail" that takes Christians from Caesarea to Nazareth, Capernaum to Jericho, and Jerusalem to Bethlehem. At each stop, they hear stories recounting the great things that happened there: where David hid from Saul, where Sarah was buried, where Jesus grew up, where he died, and where he ascended. Historical reminiscence has always been central to the Christian tradition; therefore contextualizing this history *on site* has likewise become a regular part of Christian activity. Thus the trade of guiding pilgrims has been a Middle Eastern profession almost as old as the sites themselves.

The land, however, also serves a wider purpose. *The land is the cultural stage-setting of the Bible.* Biblical stories assume we know something about altars, sheepfolds, cistern water, and the significance if the wind blows west out of the desert. To project European or American notions of farming (seed distribution) or fishing (cast and trammel nets) or travel (at night

Gary M. Burge

| BEDOUIN TENT IN WADI RUM, JORDAN

or day) onto the Bible is to immediately distance oneself from what the Bible may have intended to say.

All literature is born from within a cultural landscape. It will pick up themes and images from within that landscape, use them generously, and build a framework from which stories can be told. This is no less true for the Bible. The land and its culture, not merely the history that happened there, are an indispensable aspect of the biblical story.

This book will explore how the motifs of land and culture give rise to important and overlooked lessons in the biblical story. These are themes that every biblical writer simply assumes we understand. They are ideas such as the wilderness and water and shepherding that are picked up in biblical stories and convey messages that have been lost to us in the Western world for centuries. But the greater interest of each of these biblical writers is life: how we survive and flourish even when life is lived alongside the wilderness, even when considerable years are spent in the desert and all hope seems lost.

Each chapter will explore a motif that centers on the life of faith as it is experienced alongside the wilderness. What we will discover is that the Holy Land — or better, the biblical worldview — has already supplied us with rich metaphors that help us interpret the wilderness and succeed in it.

Chapter 2

THE LAND

THE HOLY Land itself, complete with its cities, rainfall, deserts, and culture, gives us a window into God's purposes for life. *The Promised Land is not an easy land—it is not paradise, neither today nor in biblical times.* The land has a spiritual architecture that incorporates elements that we desire (good cities with ample rainfall and rich soil) and things we would prefer to avoid (wilderness). But this is life. And when God brought his people to this land, he built into it those elements that would provide a framework for his people to understand life with him.

THE LAND AS SPIRITUAL MENTOR

Throughout the Scriptures God takes a unique interest in this land, the Holy Land, as a place of revelation. All who reside there—Jew, Muslim, or Christian—must remember that God makes a special claim on this place. Throughout the Old Testament, Israelites are reminded that even they are guests to this land. In Leviticus 25:23 God commands: "The land must not be sold permanently, because the land is mine and you reside in my land as foreigners and strangers."

The land in this respect is a unique possession of God, held for divine use. It is not a land designed for comfort or ease. I have often thought that other lands might well have served as better

JUDEAN DESERT

places for God to forge a people: places where rainfall was more abundant, where wars were less frequent, where crops grew richly and wildlife could be easily found. But in some manner this land facilitates a divine agenda; it is a land with a purpose.

Before the Israelites entered into their Promised Land, Moses told them what to expect. From the mountains east of the Jordan River, Moses compared this land to Egypt, which they had left forty years earlier, in these words:

> The land you are entering to take over is not like the land of Egypt, from which you have come, where you planted your seed and irrigated it by foot as in a vegetable garden. But the land you are crossing the Jordan to take possession of is a land of mountains and valleys that drinks rain from heaven. It is a land the LORD your God cares for; the eyes of the LORD your God are continually on it from the beginning of the year to its end. (Deut. 11:10 – 12, emphasis added)

This is a land, Moses says, that has a unique character. In Egypt the Israelites were used to the annual flooding of the Nile, around which all agriculture had been organized for millennia.

This new land, this Holy Land, would have no flooding Nile River and hence no irrigation; farmers would not be able to dig canals to channel streams to their crops. Instead, this would be a land that made demands. It must wait for God to open the heavens. It must wait for rain. This is our first clue to how the Holy Land will serve in Israel's history; *this is a land that will demand faith.*

The Land and Agriculture

ARAB FARMER PLOWING WITH
THE TOOLS OF ANTIQUITY

One of the striking features of this land is that it is a desert. While there are regions that enjoy good rainfall, such as western Galilee, a visitor is immediately struck by the lack of water. Unlike the great civilizations of antiquity found in Mesopotamia (modern Iraq) or Egypt, Israel had no river system that brought water to the center of national life. No Tigris or Euphrates, no Nile. The Jordan River system runs from the north to the south (from Galilee to the Dead Sea), but it is captive in a narrow, deep ravine that is miles from Jerusalem. Even Egypt's great cities (such as Memphis) benefited from the flooding Nile that regularly brought water and renewing silt to the fields. But Jerusalem, Hebron, and Shechem had no such source. In Deuteronomy 11

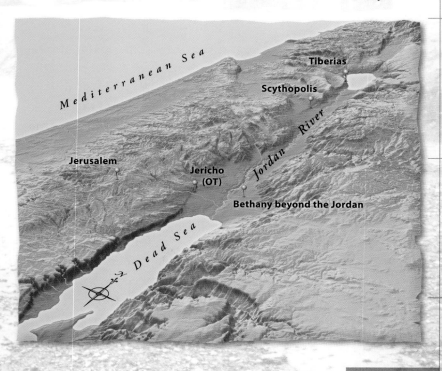

Moses is no doubt anticipating a complaint: God is bringing us to a land where we cannot engineer our water sources.

Residents of Jerusalem and surrounding villages had to develop completely different sources of water. For cities, springs were tapped, such as Jerusalem's Gihon Spring. But for farmers in the country who grew cereal crops, vines, and trees, it was necessary to wait for "rain from heaven." And in villages where there was no spring, elaborate systems of water retention were nec-

GIHON SPRING, JERUSALEM

essary. Cisterns were underground caverns carved into bedrock to catch rainwater and hold it throughout the dry summer months.

This means that Israel watched for rains carefully. It charted the rainy seasons and anticipated the threat of drought. It developed ceremonies such as the autumn Tabernacles Festival in which God was asked eagerly to deliver rain. And it valued such "water from the hand of God" (also called *living water*) as having unusual cleansing properties.

Life without a river system meant that Israel had to depend on God. The Israelites had to exhibit faith that God would sustain them agriculturally, that the rains would come, and that they would not die from drought. And when there was sin in the land, God could withhold rain or "shut the heavens" so that the land itself would withhold its blessing (2 Chron. 6:26; Isa. 5:6; Jer. 14:4; Amos 4:7).

Therefore the land's vulnerability to drought and its inability to access its water meant that faith in God was a necessary ingredient in everyday life. Today in Israel a sophisticated pumping system, the National Water Carrier, pipes water out of the Sea of Galilee and carries it south without regard for the weather or the seasons. Deep wells dug with drills now tap water tables that rest inside the mountains around Jerusalem. Israel today has engineered its way round this central feature of the land. But if these systems fail, it will only be "the windows of heaven" that will save the land and its people from drought.

ANCIENT CISTERN FROM THE ROMAN ERA, GALILEE

God's plan does not move his people into a place where comfort and safety can be engineered such as Egypt or

ISRAEL'S NATIONAL WATER CARRIER TRANSFERRING WATER FROM THE SEA OF GALILEE THROUGHOUT ISRAEL

Mesopotamia. He gives the tribes of Israel a land that is dependent on him for sustenance. It is a land where prayer for rain — as prayer for anything that sustains life — would be a regular occurrence.

The Land and Politics

The second unusual feature of the Holy Land is its lack of defined boundaries. Nations that flourish generally have a coherent experience of geography where enemies can be

JERICHO FROM THE SOUTH

kept away and an indigenous culture can flourish. Egypt, for instance, was bounded by desert on three sides and the Mediterranean Sea to the north. Its culture hugged the Nile, its religious systems were shaped by its annual flooding, and its entry points were easily guarded by fortresses. Today Britain has been shaped in part by that accident of geography, the English Channel, that forever separates it from continental Europe. America has been defined by the "isolation" of two gigantic oceans. Israel had no such fortune.

In antiquity the great nations of the world—the superpowers, perhaps—were found in Mesopotamia and Egypt. The coincidence of favorable geography brought safety and wealth to these cultures that quickly grew rich and powerful. In times of peace, trade moved comfortably between them. Caravans with over a thousand camels would leave Babylon, follow the Euphrates northwest, and frequently cross the desert to Damascus (via Tadmor or in Greek, Palmyra). Then they moved south to Galilee, along the Israelite coast, into Gaza, and on to Egypt. This route, going back to at least 2000 BC continued in use until the coming of the locomotive in the nineteenth century. We refer to it as "the Fertile Crescent."

Israel lived between Egypt and Mesopotamia, which meant that in times of peace, it could prosper. The coastal communities living on this caravan highway could benefit from trade,

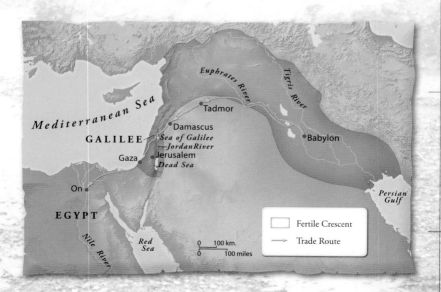

could tax travelers, and could even sell them provisions. For this reason, in peacetime Israel edged down from the hills of Judea and competed with the Philistines for influence along the great "trade highway." But in times of war—such as the Egyptian Shishak's campaign against Israel (1 Kings 11:40; 14:25)—Israel withdrew back into the mountains of Judea because its cities could be devastated. The "highway" linking the two superpowers of Egypt and Mesopotamia ran right through coastal Israel. In one season it hosted a trade caravan; another season it might see a hostile army 10,000 strong.

This tension of geography and politics continued to play out in Israel's fortunes. Alexander the Great used this highway in the fourth century BC. The Roman general Pompey did the same in the first century BC. All varieties of empires for the past two thousand years have done the same: Byzantine, Muslim, Crusader, Turkish, even British armies used the highway. And in each case, Jerusalem found itself on the "must conquer" city list of general after general.

Israel lacked the safe buffer of ocean or desert. It was on a crossroads, which meant that its political fortunes were always in jeopardy. It enjoyed no natural geographical boundary, no cohesive land mass, or no defining location. At least the Phoe-

"THE TREASURY" IN PETRA, JORDAN

nicians (in today's Lebanon) exploited their coastline and had the great Lebanon Mountains as a wall against Syria. The Nabateans (in today's Jordan) took advantage of deep, cavernous valleys tucked into desert mountain ranges.

In this setting, how would Israel find political security? *This was not safety that could be engineered.* Egyptian forts blocking all roads south of Gaza effectively protected that nation. Israel could build no such strategy.

Therefore this land required one thing. It required its people to trust God for their political welfare. The great temptation throughout the Old Testament was whether Israel would make alliances with other small tribal nations who lived nearby. Such coalitions were the hoped-for solution to local insecurity and weakness. And in times of crisis, Israel's greatest leaders called God's people back to renew their commitments to him. Second Kings 18 – 19 tells us about King Hezekiah, when violent Assyrian kings from Mesopotamia threatened to overrun the land. The challenge was to rely on God's protection and not place ultimate trust in political alliances with pagan nations.

Therefore, the land demands faith on yet another level. No national strategy, no economic policy, no army or model of government will permanently guarantee security. This land mentors its occupants to trust God with their histories.

The Land and Cultural Assimilation

Because Israel lived at a crossroads and because a variety of other, similar cultures lived nearby, the land has never been empty. Before the Israelites arrived, Canaanites lived there. The Philistines were to the west, Midianites to the south, Syria was north, while Ammon, Moab, and Edom were rivals from the east.

Before Israel entered and conquered this land, the nation was warned again and again that cultural assimilation would be its supreme temptation: "When you enter the land the LORD your God is giving you, do not learn to imitate the detestable ways of the nations there" (Deut. 18:9). Israel was fully aware of the things these cultures did. The ancient world commonly practiced sorcery, looked for omens, consulted the dead,

GATE AT DAN

developed fertility rituals, and even sacrificed children to their gods (Deut. 18:10–12). A cultural consensus from Egypt to Syria no doubt affirmed that such activities generated power or wealth or security.

Under Joshua's leadership, Israel conquered Canaan and began its settlement of the land. But despite this conquest, cultural pressures remained. Israel did not enjoy a monolithic cultural dominance. This reality is illustrated easily in the story of the tribe of Dan. Rejecting its tribal allotment, Dan left for the north, recruited its own priests from within the pagan culture, and set up its own worship system (Judg. 18). Much later, when the nation of Israel split into northern and southern kingdoms, it took only moments for pagan religious instincts to resurface (see Jeroboam in 1 Kings 12). Israel was constantly rubbing shoulders with nations who refused to acknowledge God and his people. As the prophets warned, assimilation with their ways meant losing the benefits of a relationship with God.

Hundreds of years later, the same temptation returned. Greek civilization came to Israel with a vengeance in the fourth century BC, and again God's people struggled. Speaking Greek might be safe enough, but should they translate their Scriptures into Greek? And what about Greek stadiums and theaters and temples? It was the same struggle: the crossroads life of the Holy Land constantly forced Israel to rethink its commitment to God's covenant and assess when life alongside another culture could be dangerous.

For some Jews, living in the Greek and Roman empires presented no problems. By the New Testament era, huge Jewish communities thrived in Alexandria (Egypt) and Babylon (Mesopotamia). But their decision to live "away from the land" came with genuine risks to their Jewish cultural and religious identity.

The lesson of the land brought a persistent truth that each generation needed to revisit. Can faith be compromised when people of faith live with cultural and religious diversity? When culture is homogenous, when there is little to challenge beliefs, rituals, and traditions, faith seems easier. But God placed his people in a land where this luxury did not exist, where faith had to be defined, examined, and reembraced on a regular basis.

THE LAND AND FAITH

Life in this land (or any other) is an ongoing struggle for faith. It is a struggle with temptation. With testing. Will rainfall bring crops that will sustain life from year to year? Will I have prosperity or want? Should I trust governments, political ideologies, and militaries with my future or listen to divine counsel? And how is it that my own renewal must be continually sharpened by those who surround me and challenge me?

It is interesting that before Jesus began his ministry, he found himself in the wilderness, in the land, *tested*. Could he trust God to sustain him, to make him secure, to define his life? Would he be a man of faith? Or would he try to use his own power to meet his needs?

Chapter 3

WILDERNESS

Deuteronomy 6–8; Matthew 4

THE WILDERNESS (or desert) of the Holy Land is one of this land's most characteristic features. First-time visitors are stopped short, holding their breaths, squinting at distant brown horizons that shimmer in the heat. Intrigued, you want to step closer, to imagine yourself wandering alone—in a caravan perhaps—exploring a moonscape terrain, moving from monastery to oasis and back. You want to locate thousand-year-old ruins that still hold stories.

But another voice inside warns you to beware, to take water and a map and preferably a guide. You instinctively know that if you walk over the next hill, every hill might look the same and there might be no coming back.

THE WILDERNESS TERRAIN

Every region around the world has natural features that set it apart. When I moved to Chicago some years ago, I immediately knew that I had entered a place quite different from my native California. The American Midwest gave new meaning to the notion of "flat terrain." It struck me as odd that people could spend a lifetime without mountains and a nearby ocean. Lake Michigan, they argued, was as good as any sea—and to an extent I agreed. I had never seen a lake on that scale in my

WILDERNESS OF PARAN

entire life. A student of mine traveled to Colorado one semester to attend another college, and when she returned I was eager to hear her report. "How was the scenery? Were the mountains beautiful?" Her response: "The mountains were fine," she said, "except they got in the way of the view." Only a native Midwesterner could think along those lines.

Then there was the weather. I was both amused and worried when the temperature dropped below twenty degrees for the first time. When it hit zero I wondered if even the car would work. Or if metal would break. Soon you learn how to wear a hat and keep track of your gloves. And you buy a coat—a serious coat.

Anyone who grows up in Chicago finds these features of life commonplace. And they would listen to me with a smile, wondering if I'd mastered the skills of the snow blower and driving on snow-covered roads. To an outsider, winters like these don't remind you of cross-country skiing. Winters like these feel threatening, confusing, miserable even. It takes time and effort to understand them.

The Land and Wilderness

The one indisputable fact about life in the Holy Land is the desert. As Lake Michigan is to Chicago, so the desert is to Israel.

It is always there, just east of every major city in the central hills. A drive from Jerusalem to Bethlehem skirts its edges, and off to the left for miles one catches glimpses of nothing but desolation.

The eastern deserts are not the rolling sand dunes one imagines in places like the Sahara. These are rock-strewn, eroded wildernesses. Outside Bethlehem they create rocky scarps and ancient canyons, seemingly impassible valleys that only the skilled Arab will know how to cross. This desert moves east from the cities of Israel, continues a steep descent to the Jordan River, climbs up to a high desert plateau in Jordan—then continues for hundreds of miles. Beyond are the great deserts of Arabia and to the north, Iraq. Sometimes the features are barren, windswept emptiness; at other times (such as eastern Jordan) one meets a sea of volcanic stone, strewn from the blast of an ancient volcano. (Such black basalt "seas" are known to every nomad in the region whose camels refuse to cross them.)

EN GEDI

Therefore, life in every biblical city—Hebron, Bethlehem, Jerusalem, Shechem—was defined by its proximity to this wilderness. From Jerusalem the wilderness is just behind the Mount of Olives. When Saul was in pursuit of David, David fled southeast, slipping into the wilderness for safety, making his way eventually to the oasis of En Gedi (1 Sam. 24:1). When travelers in antiquity wanted to walk from Jerusalem to Galilee, they often entered the wilderness on an old road (nicely carved by the Romans) and headed to Jericho. From there it was about seventy-five miles north to the great inland Sea of Galilee. When Jesus was tested after his baptism, the

Spirit drove him (Mark 1:12) into this wilderness for forty days. He was tested between Jerusalem and Jericho.

The Wilderness and the Bible

It should come as no surprise that words referring to this wilderness appear in the English Bible over four hundred times. This is a motif that cannot be ignored by any literature coming from this region. As northern European children tell stories about forests and snows, so Middle Eastern children know stories about the desert, about travel and danger, about jeopardy and heroism. Stories of camels and oases and mystery. The desert still strikes a deep chord with every Middle Easterner—Jew, Muslim, and Christian. From Abraham to Paul, from Muhammad to Saladin, from Aladdin to Lawrence of Arabia, the desert wilderness shapes their identities.

Abraham was known as a wilderness traveler who crossed the Syrian deserts to arrive in Canaan. The striking thing about his story is that God calls him not simply to a new place, but to a new life: he now has an address, a land, a destination rather than wandering. He moves from being a man with caravan and tent to a man whose tent now resides in mountains assigned to him by God.

OASIS OF KADESH BARNEA

Z. Radovan/www.BibleLandPictures.com

The tribes of Israel likewise left Egypt and crossed the deserts, this time in the south. After two years among the desert tribe of Midianites at Mount Sinai, Moses led them north through the wilderness of Paran to the oasis of Kadesh Barnea, and from there they wandered for thirty-eight more years. These people were not wandering through trees—as Moses described later: "Then, as the Lord our God commanded us, we set out from Horeb [Sinai] and went toward the hill country of the Amorites through all that vast and dreadful wilderness that you have seen, and so we reached Kadesh Barnea" (Deut. 1:19). It was a terrifying experience, filled with dangers. Moses' descriptions become even more grim: "[Remember our God, who] led you through the vast and dreadful wilderness, that thirsty and waterless land, with its venomous snakes and scorpions" (Deut. 8:15).

The desert experience of Israel was formative, repeated in many liturgical refrains, to remind Israel of its heritage. When a family came to the tabernacle altar to sacrifice the firstfruits of their harvest, they were to recite: "My father was a wandering Aramean, and he went down to Egypt . . ." (Deut. 26:5, Aramean refers to the people of Abraham and the patriarchs). The collective memory of desert life gave new poignancy to settled life and hopefully filled the Israelites with gratitude for the good things that came from their fields.

The wilderness likewise figures into the stories of the New Testament. When Jesus was born, Herod the Great immediately tried to destroy him through an attack on Bethlehem. Mary and Joseph knew just what to do. They fled to the wilderness (just as David had done). They traveled south this time, eventually coming to Egypt, and they waited there until their attacker was dead. This journey was a classic desert journey, a flight seeking refuge from the villain. Few pursuers would follow anyone into the desert.

The wilderness motif appeared again when Jesus was tested for forty days (an echo of Israel's forty years in the wilderness). It returned again in many of his parables. The good Samaritan met a man who was traveling between Jerusalem and Jericho—in the wilderness. The question each potential rescuer had to ask was whether helping the wounded traveler might jeopardize his or her life or status.

ISRAEL'S DUAL OUTLOOK

The Bible represents the wilderness with seemingly opposite views. The same is true today. On the one hand, it is a place of genuine danger, and people who live near it would never think of entering it except under duress. Stories of romance and mystery are matched with stories of tragedy and loss. Israelis and Palestinians alike can tell of people hiking through the wilderness, getting lost or attacked, and never coming home again.

On the other hand, Arab culture speaks of the desert with great fondness, telling stories that imply that all of the great heroes of their history spring from the desert. Christian Arabs will refer to the desert ascetics — monks who once lived in impossible desert caves with severe austerity to recreate the extreme spirituality they thought belonged to the earliest Christians. The eccentric St. Simon Stylites of Syria (388 – 459) comes to mind. Not only did he live in the desert without food, but spent a good deal of his life (thirty-six years) atop a fifty-foot pillar in northern Syria (in the town of Qal at Simân [Arabic] or Qalat Sam'an [English]).

Muslim Arabs refer to conquering heroes such as Saladin (or Salah al-Din), the twelfth-century Muslim general who defeated the Crusaders in 1187. The shadows of such desert heroes are long: Saladin was from the village of Tikrit (Iraq) on the Tigris River. Iraq's notorious Saddam Hussein never tired of reminding the Muslim world that Tikrit was his home as well. The implication of heroism was obvious. He was the new Saladin, now driving out the Western powers again.

In this culture, the wilderness is both respected and feared. It is the source of

PAINTING OF
STYLITE PILLAR

adventure and excitement—a place where remarkable things happen—and also a place where tragedy strikes. People are changed in the desert, but they also die there.

The Danger of the Wilderness

To read wilderness stories from the Bible and miss the implied sense of danger is to miss something vital. The book of Exodus describes the Israelite departure from Egypt and their dramatic exit through the sea—but we rarely read further. Behind them the sea closed. Before them is—nothing but rock, sand, and heat. They are in the Wilderness of Shur (Ex. 15:22) and for three days they cannot find water. And when they locate some, it is undrinkable. No wonder that within three days, complaints echo throughout the Israelite camp.

But God is with them. Through Moses he shows them that he can make bitter water drinkable (15:25) and that he can lead them to an oasis with a dozen flowing springs and seventy palm trees (the oasis of Elim, 15:27).

Israel continues through this region and passes south into the Desert of Sin (16:1). Water and food are still missing, and the story makes clear that if Moses does not know what he is doing, if God does not provide for these tribes, they will die at

Tim Kimberley/www.istockphoto.com

WILDERNESS OF ZIN

once. Soon miracles begin to happen and manna and quail feed them, but this is never under Israelite control. God sustains in the desert and no human solutions can be devised.

This story—and others like it—underscores one theme: *the wilderness can destroy anyone.* And were it not for God's intervention, all human hope will be lost.

Moses' anxiety about leading his people north to the Holy Land is evident in his recruitment of a man named Hobab. Despite God's assurances to lead them day and night (with pillars of cloud and fire), Moses urges Hobab, his new brother-in-law, to serve as desert guide: "You know where we should camp in the wilderness, and you can be our eyes" (Num. 10:31). The wilderness is too dangerous to take any chances, and so Hobab relents and joins the tribal caravan.

The dangers of the wilderness are clear: no water, no food, becoming lost and disoriented, attacks by nomadic raiders or bandits, and in some areas in antiquity, the threat of wild animals. These dangers are native to the lore of the desert. In the good Samaritan story the desert traveler is attacked by thieves (Luke 10). The danger of the desert is evident in the reassurances given in Psalm 23 that the sheep are guided in the wilderness. Finding "green pastures," "quiet waters," "right paths," and the safety of a shepherd's "rod and . . . staff" all serve as comfort for the sheep, who cannot survive alone in the wilderness.

The Appeal of the Wilderness

Now here is the surprise. The same wilderness that threatens is also the wilderness that forms Israel's major leaders. Virtually every major biblical character—Old Testament and New Testament—spends some time in the wilderness and is shaped by experiences there. Abraham came from the wilderness and was called from it to settle in Canaan. Jacob fled from his brother Esau and ran east—into the wilderness—where God met him. Moses fled Egypt after killing an Egyptian guard and in the desert of Sinai encountered God, accepted his mission, and returned to Egypt. Israel spent forty years in the desert immediately after its birth as a nation at Sinai. David was a wilderness shepherd outside Bethlehem before he was selected as

Israel's king—and when Saul pursued him, he returned to that wilderness he knew so intimately.

Prophets knew the wilderness well. After Elijah killed the prophets of Baal on Mount Carmel, he fled—to the southern wilderness. When he came to the region of Mount Sinai, God met him. Amos was from the village of Tekoa, a remote desert village southeast of Bethlehem.

Even as we read the New Testament, parallel themes emerge. John the Baptist conducted his ministry along the Jordan River, which required people to cross the wilderness to join him in this remote region. Jesus began his ministry after John baptized him and he had spent forty days in the wilderness between Jericho and Jerusalem. Even Paul, following his conversion on the road to Damascus, entered the deserts of Arabia and spent three years there before he emerged in Jerusalem as an articulate and confident Christian.

The "wilderness" suddenly moves from being an incidental element in biblical stories to an important motif bearing serious theological weight. God uses the wilderness as a place to form his people. There is indeed something threatening here, but also something constructive. People are silenced in the wilderness. They see their own vulnerability and their need to depend on God with renewed clarity. They intuit at once that life is tenuous and that without some help, without some intervention, life will be lost.

When people enter the wilderness for the first time, they feel their anxieties quicken. Yet at the same time they are drawn to its silence and its austerity. It is no wonder that within 250 years of Jesus' death, a Christian monastic movement had formed in Egypt and moved quickly to the Judean wilderness to recreate this experience. Today many of their monasteries are still living communities.

THE WILDERNESS AND FAITH

The wilderness is a theological symbol for flight and deprivation. For suffering and loss. For vulnerability and helplessness. For dislocation and confusion. But it is also the spiritual setting where renewal takes place, where men and women *in the midst of their crisis* discover something about God they had not known before.

When Israel completed its forty years in the wilderness with Moses, he led the people to a high plateau in current-day western Jordan. They could look across the Jordan Valley and see that good promise of land God was extending to them. But he would not let them possess it yet. Instead, he interpreted the meaning of the wilderness experience they had just completed. Deuteronomy is his recitation of the law once given at Sinai, now reinforced and extended to new areas before their entry into the Holy Land. And in this book, in chapters 6–10, Moses interprets the function of wilderness experiences.

Moses reminds Israel of many things: their sacred commitment made at Sinai to the covenant; their promise to remain pure and unpolluted by Canaanite culture, their national ideal of building a nation of righteousness and goodness. And then he tells them to never forget what the wilderness was for:

> Remember how the LORD your God led you all the way in the wilderness these forty years, to humble and test you in order to know what was in your heart, whether or not you would keep his commands. He humbled you, causing you to hunger and then feeding you with manna, which neither you nor your ancestors had known, to teach you that people do not live on bread alone but on every word that comes from the mouth of the LORD. Your clothes did not wear out and your feet did not swell during these forty years. Know then in your heart that as a man disciplines his son, so the LORD your God disciplines you. (Deut. 8:2–5)

Wilderness experiences can either become remarkable opportunities for renewal and faith, or they can become opportunities for bitterness and anger. In a word, when each person stands in the wilderness of their own desolation, they must decide how to respond. Many Israelites never arrived at the Holy Land but instead died in the wilderness. The wilderness story is punctuated with accounts of men and women exhibiting marked anger and resentment that Moses and his God were not doing a better job of managing things.

Others were willing to be silent and learn. When Jesus was in his wilderness for forty days, Satan tempted him with numerous ways to resolve the difficulty of his own vulnerability. In each case, Jesus responded by citing texts from Deuteronomy 6–10, Israel's manual for wilderness life.

The wilderness, then, is an opportunity to hear things we have never heard before, to discover what lies at the very center of our souls. It is not fun, nor is it easy. But oddly, God delights in speaking in the wilderness. In the sterility and austerity of the desert, in this silence provoked by deprivation, God is heard. This is precisely what happened to Elijah (1 Kings 19). In the wilderness of his despair, when he finally sits beneath a tree and gives up, an angel speaks to him and feeds him. After forty days of more travel, he hides in a cave at Mount Sinai and suddenly he hears the Lord speak, "What are you doing here, Elijah?" And from that moment a new conversation begins.

The Bible offers no account of a godly man or woman avoiding the wilderness. It is a severe mercy, but a mercy nevertheless. The wilderness experience is where we discover something about ourselves — and God sees what is truly in our hearts. It is here where his simple provisions of water and manna and quail suddenly are seen for their beauty and wonder. And it is here where we might hear his voice in ways unheard before.

TRANS-JORDANIAN PLATEAU

Chapter 4

SHEPHERDS

Psalm 23; Ezekiel 34; John 10

MEN AND women can live in the wilderness. In some cases, they will be nomads who move from oasis to oasis. In other cases, they enter the wilderness temporarily in order to pasture their animals. Today as well as in antiquity it is not uncommon to see a Palestinian shepherd from a nearby village leading large groups of sheep and goats across the rocky terrain.

On more than one occasion I've been in the desert east of Jerusalem, in southern Syria, or in Jordan and seen one of these shepherding troupes. Two things always surprise me: the desolate terrain where they live and the apparent skill they must have in order to survive. They are purposeful. And their sheep look healthy. I remember once stopping my walk and simply sitting down as a distant shepherd and his forty sheep moved across my horizon, disappearing silently into a deep canyon. The lesson seemed obvious: there are skills that permit someone to master the wilderness, and shepherds like this man had them.

THE SHEPHERD AND THE WILDERNESS

Shepherd stories abound in the Bible. Not only is God known as the shepherd of his people (Ps. 23:1), but Israel's kings, beginning with David (1 Sam 16:19), were known as shepherds of the nation (Ezek. 34:23). Taking care of sheep—feeding them,

SHEEP IN A FIELD

protecting them, leading them — was such a common feature of life in antiquity that it is natural to find this metaphor in biblical literature. The

DESERT OASIS

good king was a good shepherd; bad kings were bad shepherds.

The same is true today. I remember hiking alone once into the wilderness east from Jerusalem on my way to Jericho. I bypassed the modern Israeli highway in order to experience what it was like to travel this route in antiquity. I followed a deep valley system (the Wadi Qilt) where there were monasteries, some deserted, one inhabited. It was a desolate scene and (for good reason) no one else was there. But I rounded a corner and surprised a flock of sheep. Four Arab boys were lying in the shade of a cliff, playing cards, drinking tea, and — throwing rocks at their sheep. They expected no visitors.

When they heard me coming, they must have thought I was their father since they immediately sprang to life, kicked over their tea, and began to look dutiful. It was evident they knew they were in the wrong. Their sheep were scattered far, they were being neglected, and these boys were violating deep values in their shepherding culture. They were bad shepherds.

This wilderness is inhospitable to sheep unless they

SHEPHERD WITH SHEEP IN JUDEAN HILLS

have an expert guide. There seems to be no water or vegetation. A wrong turn can send the flock off cliffs a thousand feet high. Poor directions can lead you in circles until exhaustion, dehydration, or starvation overtakes you. It's like hiking in the middle of the Rocky Mountains during winter. Every direction looks the same and with time, you know you might not make it out.

But the culture also knows good shepherds. In 1989 during the first Palestinian uprising against the Israeli military occupation, soldiers came to a poor village near Bethlehem and demanded the people pay the taxes they were refusing to pay. (Such taxes, these people argued, simply financed their occupation.) To punish the village, the officer in charge rounded up all of the village's animals (chiefly sheep and goats) and

A SHEPHERD WATERING HIS HERD OF SHEEP AND GOATS IN THE FOOTHILLS OF JUDEA

placed them in huge barbed-wire pen. In a famous incident, a poor woman came to the officer begging that her animals be released. Her husband had been imprisoned and her animals were all she had. The Israeli laughed, saying that finding her twelve animals inside a pen of thousands would be impossible. But, she argued, if she could identify her twelve and get them without disruption, could she? He was intrigued and gave in.

The woman brought forward her ten-year-old son. He stood at the now-opened barbed wire gate, pulled out a flute, and began to play a simple tune. Suddenly sheep began looking up from every corner of the pen. Continuing to play the boy began walking away and before long, twelve sheep were at his heels following him home. The Israelis were so impressed they broke into applause, shut the gate, and announced that no one else could try that trick. This boy was a good shepherd. He knew his sheep, and his sheep knew him.

GOOD SHEPHERDS OF THE WILDERNESS

For thousands of years, this has been a culture that has understood sheep. Here people understand what it means to be a reliable, competent shepherd, particularly if work is being done in the hostile eastern wilderness. The skills are public and handed down from generation to generation. And because of this, shepherding can become a poignant metaphor for good and bad leadership. The word group is picked up over three hundred times in the Bible and often refers to the good shepherding of God. After describing Israel's exodus from Egypt, Psalm 78 continues:

> But he brought his people out like a flock;
>> he led them like sheep through the wilderness.
> He guided them safely, so they were unafraid;
>> but the sea engulfed their enemies.
> And so he brought them to the border of his holy land,
>> to the hill country his right hand had taken. (Ps. 78:52–54)

Ezekiel 34 provides a startling counterpoint. Here the prophet outlines the failures of Israel's kings and leaders but does so with a shepherding motif:

> Therefore, you shepherds, hear the word of the LORD: As surely as I live, declares the Sovereign LORD, because my flock lacks a shepherd and so has been plundered and has become food for all the wild animals, and because my shepherds did not search for my flock but cared for themselves rather than for my flock, therefore, you shepherds, hear the word of the LORD: This is what the Sovereign LORD says: I am against the shepherds and will hold them accountable for my flock. I will remove them from tending the flock so that the shepherds can no longer feed themselves. I will rescue my flock from their mouths, and it will no longer be food for them.

Competent Shepherds

So what are the skills a competent shepherd had to master? Psalm 23 provides a remarkable outline of the skills deemed necessary before anyone can lead a flock of sheep into the wilderness. Without these skills the sheep will die; with them, they will return home to the village.

> The LORD is my shepherd, I lack nothing.
>> He makes me lie down in green pastures,
> he leads me beside quiet waters,

he refreshes my soul.
He guides me along the right paths
for his name's sake.
Even though I walk
through the darkest valley,
I will fear no evil,
for you are with me;
your rod and your staff,
they comfort me.

Here we have the beginning of a list. (1) First, competent shepherds need to know how to locate food in the wilderness. To the untrained eye, the wilderness has nothing. But there are springs to be found where grass grows, and in certain seasons just following rain, succulent plants are abundant. Here the psalm praises God not only because he can feed his sheep in the wilderness, but also because he can find green pastures—a rarity.

(2) Competent shepherds must be able to locate water. Rainfall is scarce since the mountains of Judea create a rain shadow to the east. Los Angeles, for instance, has an average annual rainfall of twenty inches; Chicago gets thirty-two. The wilderness around Jericho gets five inches of annual rain (like Palm Springs, California). This means that locating water from springs is essential. The competent shepherd does this, and he creates a pool of quiet water from the desert spring.

(3) The competent shepherd knows his directions. He can find water and pasturage and get the sheep home. He has memorized the numerous paths that crisscross the wilderness; he knows which ones are dangerous; he can tell how many hours it will take to return the flock before nightfall and selects his route accordingly. The "right paths" must not be spiritualized (some translations read "paths of righteousness"—these are routes that will keep the sheep safe so that they will not get lost or harmed. All of this work—this feeding, watering, guiding—this competence, is what enables the sheep to be safe and restored.

(4) Finally, the competent shepherd knows that this wilderness is dangerous for other reasons as well. In antiquity the

SHEPHERD WITH STAFF

wilderness had wild animals and bandits ready to make short work of the flock. In a desert where food was scarce, to lead fifty sheep among predators such as wolves, jackals, hyenas, and lions was a dangerous business. Therefore the competent shepherd entered the wilderness armed. A wooden staff, a club, and sling stones were common. (David, for instance, could hit Goliath with a sling stone thanks to years of practice in the wilderness.) The shepherd needed to be ready for the lethal defense of the flock, when he stood between them and the attacker, and heaving stones and swinging an oak staff were all that would keep him and his animals alive.

The skills of the competent shepherd were well known. His reputation to guide, feed, water, and protect sheep generally meant that the village might cluster together sheep and place them under his care. If there were more sheep than fifty, he would have an assistant. This helps explain Jesus' parable in Luke 15:3−7. In this story a hundred sheep are in the wilderness and one is lost. No competent shepherd would leave the ninety-nine alone in the wilderness to find the one lost animal! This would be neglect. Instead, he leaves the ninety-nine with his assistants (assumed in the parable) and hunts for the lost sheep so that not one is lost from his care.

Noble Shepherds

Jesus grew up alongside this shepherding culture and he understood the wilderness well. And he was happy to be viewed as a shepherd taking care of God's people. At one point, Jesus arrived in Galilee by boat. Mark comments: "When Jesus landed and saw a large crowd, he had compassion on them, because they were like sheep without a shepherd" (Mark 6:34). Jesus gathered them together in groups of fifties and hundreds and made them sit on "green grass" (6:39–40); then he fed them. He is the good shepherd of Israel.

In John 10, however, Jesus picks up the shepherding theme in full. He does this at an important Jewish feast: the Festival of Hanukkah. Here Jewish priests reflected on the leadership failures of the past (during the turbulent Maccabean period) and read aloud Ezekiel 34, where the prophet outlines the deficient "shepherding" of Israel's priests. It is in this setting, while Jerusalem is studying "priestly shepherding," that Jesus announces, "I am the good shepherd" (John 10:11).

It is important not to overly sentimentalize the image given here. This is not a portrait of a kindly man holding

| POSSIBLE LOCATION OF THE FEEDING OF THE MULTITUDE

cuddly lambs. This is not the usual Greek word for good (*agathos*); rather, the text uses *kalos*, and we should translate it "noble." The shepherd's job was severe, tiring, and hazardous. The point of contrast here is the "bad shepherd" or the hired hand, who is distinguished by his lack of commitment to the sheep (John 10:12). When danger comes, he flees (v. 12) and the flock is attacked. His own self-preservation, his own self-interest (he "cares nothing for the sheep," v. 13b), characterizes his career; this element no doubt refers directly to the leaders of Israel graphically chastised during the Hanukkah Festival. The noble or good shepherd, by contrast, "owns the sheep" (v. 12a), which speaks to his unique, passionate commitment to them.

John 10 suggests that in Jesus' mind, there are features to the work of the noble shepherd that characterize him and that would have been recognized in his day. This shepherd—in addition to the four skills of the competent shepherd (food, water, direction, defense)—has two more skills that set him apart.

(1) These shepherds know their sheep intimately. They do not simply know the terrain, they know how their flock will react. They understand the endurance of particular sheep. They know if any are ill or wounded. They listen with skilled ears, knowing when the flock is agitated or when it is at rest. It is the quality of their life together that sets this shepherd apart. And when they lead, they sing to them or play a flute for them (as we have seen), and the sheep are comforted by the familiarity of these sounds. These shepherds know instinctively that wise leaders cannot push a flock of sheep; rather, sheep must be led.

With this idea in mind, Jesus says (of himself): I go ahead of them, my sheep follow me because they know my voice—they will never follow a stranger; in fact they will flee from him because they do not recognize his voice (10:4–5, 14). Again it is Jesus' intimate knowledge of his flock, knowing their sounds, and his flock's intimate knowledge of his voice, that make him different.

(2) In this passage, however, Jesus adds a final element to the profile of the noble shepherd. Not only can he lead his sheep to food, water, good trails, and safety; not only does he

STONE SHEEPFOLD IN THE WILDERNESS

know *his* sheep utterly well, but also in defending his sheep, he is willing to lay down his life. This is unexpected.

In the evening, if the shepherd decides to keep the flock in the wilderness and not return to the village, he will drive the sheep into a sheepfold. These are commonly at the far end of a canyon where a low stone wall creates a small enclosure. The wall is topped with thorny branches and there is one entrance. After the sheep are led up the canyon and into the sheepfold, the entrance is closed with more bushes. Or the shepherd might himself sleep at the door. Thus, Jesus can refer to himself as "the gate" of the enclosure: "I am the gate; whoever enters through me will be saved. They will come in and go out, and find pasture" (John 10:9). And he says that anyone or anything that enters the fold by avoiding the gate is dangerous (10:1). Thus, no one gains access to the sheep without going through the shepherd.

If the flock is under attack, the shepherd has choices. An incompetent shepherd may either flee for his life (John 10:12–13) or take a young lamb and toss it to the wolves, hoping to save the flock. But the noble shepherd will do no such thing. Every sheep, even the youngest lambs, are known and valued. He will stand at the entrance of the fold, keeping between his

Todd Bolen/www.BiblePlaces.com

sheep and danger and fight to the death (10:15, 17–18). It is this mortal combat, this willingness to stand firm in the brink, that sets the noble shepherd apart from every other. "I am the good shepherd. The good shepherd lays down his life for the sheep. The hired hand is not the shepherd and does not own the sheep. So when he sees the wolf coming, he abandons the sheep and runs away" (10:11–12).

THE SHEPHERD, THE WILDERNESS, AND FAITH

The motif of the wilderness expressed one central truth: the wilderness is the place where God's people are forged, where they learn about their vulnerabilities, where they rediscover his voice. No great man or woman of God will avoid the wilderness.

But now we learn something more. While God may send us into the wilderness, we do not go there alone. The Lord is not a shepherd who cares for sheep in domesticated pastures. *He is a wilderness shepherd*. He leads his people through the wilderness, going there with them. And above all, he has the requisite skills and the noble character to bring his people through conditions that they might not manage on their own. He prepares a table there. He finds green grass and pooled water. And his skill permits him to locate safe passage, where to us there are only peril and dread. If this is the case, we can understand why for his people, for his sheep, "goodness and love" will follow such a journey (Ps. 23:6).

Sheep have an instinct for danger and safety. And there is no doubt that a sheep that strays from the flock, disregards the safety of the nighttime sheepfold, and fails to keep an eye on the leading shepherd will find the wilderness impossible. The severity of the wilderness exceeds any sheep's skill. Only a skilled and noble shepherd can lead his flock through it.

Chapter 5

ROCK

Deuteronomy 32; Joshua 4; Luke 6:46–49

THE PALESTINIANS have an old story they like to tell. When God was making the world, he assigned the angel Gabriel to distribute stones and rock. Gabriel did this diligently and flew here and there with a very large sack of stones on his back. But when he was flying over the mountains around Jerusalem, the sack broke and the entire load fell.

The wilderness is a deserted place filled with rock: stones weighing tons protruding from cliffs; sharp, palm-sized rocks on every trail; stones forming walls, houses, and farming terraces. This is a natural part of the landscape—and it becomes a poignant metaphor for anyone who experiences life alongside the wilderness.

ROCK AND ANCIENT CULTURE

The Holy Land is a world where stones played an important role in the culture. The wilderness, as we have seen, is not a world of flat, sandy expanses; it is a "rocky wilderness." Loose stones lie everywhere. Stone-throwing as a skill is just one example of their use. This is how David killed Goliath. And today this is a native reflex of Palestinians engaged in street-fighting with Israelis.

The reason for this terrain is that the backbone of the country is a massive limestone mountain that has eroded century

ROCK FORMATION IN THE JUDEAN WILDERNESS
Phillip Spears

ROCKS IN THE WILDERNESS

by century. Stones break up underground, percolate to the surface, and lie exposed. Further erosion of this limestone produces a remarkably rich soil (called *terra rosa*), but with it is the ongoing problem of rock debris. Thus farmers must always be at work, clearing their fields and collecting fist-sized stones to make hillside terraces or stone walls.

In the parable of the sower, Jesus refers to a man casting seed and some of it "falls among rocks." This is simply a part of the field that needs to be cleared further. In the ancient world walking can be treacherous, especially at night. So Jesus says, "Are there not twelve hours of daylight? Those who walk in the daytime will not stumble, for they see by this world's light. It is when people walk at night that they stumble, for they have no light" (John 11:9–10). Paul uses the same image: the Jews "stumbled over the stumbling stone. As it is written: 'See, I lay in Zion a stone that causes people to stumble and a rock that makes them fall'" (Rom. 9:32–33).

The central place of rock shows up in a variety of other ways. For instance, building was done with stone. Brick-making was a skill cultivated in Egypt and Mesopotamia but not in Israel (except in parts of northern Galilee). Brick-making recalled slavery and exile (Ex. 1:14; Isa. 9:10). Walls built with stacked stones were common in Israel in

REMAINS OF THE "WINEMAKERS HOUSE," BETHSAIDA, GALILEE

the Old Testament, and this gave way eventually to cut stone, which made a more stable, reliable structure.

Jesus' trade may well have exceeded carpentry (Matt. 13:55; Mark 6:3). The Greek word *tekton* does refer to those who work in wood, but it can also refer to "one who builds" and, thus, can imply a worker in stone. During Jesus' adolescence, a major stone

ANCIENT STONE WALL, MACHAERUS, JORDAN

city called Sepphoris was under construction just north of Nazareth. It would have been natural for Jesus and Joseph to find work as stone-cutters there.

A good home builder must know the advantages of stone. Homes were not built on topsoil, which always collected at the bottom of valleys. The builder looked for places where the bedrock was exposed, chiseled a flat area, and then stacked cut foundation stones to create the perimeter of the house. Such homes—anchored to bedrock and designed with cut limestone—were virtually unmovable. This becomes another good analogy for a parable of Jesus. The wise builder does

AERIAL VIEW OF SEPPHORIS

OSSUARY

just this: he builds on bedrock, not on soil (or sand), which is unstable—and this is compared to a person who hears Jesus' words and obeys him (Luke 6:46–49).

Tombs must therefore be chiseled out of bedrock, and today large complex underground caverns can be found throughout the mountains. Stone burial boxes (called ossuaries) received the bones of decomposed bodies and were stored in such tombs.

Water was stored in underground cisterns cut by chiselers into the bedrock, then lined with plaster so that they would hold precious water. Stone-cutting developed into such a fine art that the development of public buildings in the Greek and Roman eras produced stunning examples that still remain today. For example, Herod the Great's refurbished temple in Jerusalem hosted a royal porch on its south perimeter. Its roof was supported with 160 decorated limestone columns, each weighing five tons. Remnants of them have recently been unearthed in Jerusalem excavations.

GOD AND ROCK

If rock forms an essential part of the terrain and culture of the Holy Land, it should not surprise us to see that rock likewise appears in the literature of the Bible. The Bible refers to all of the building, farming, burial, and water-storage skills outlined above. But it also picks up the terminology of "rock" and employs it as a metaphor. For instance, the psalms refer to God as "a rock" with marked frequency (at least thirty times; ephasis added below):

> The LORD is my rock, my fortress and my deliverer;
>> my God is my rock, in whom I take refuge,
>> my shield and the horn of my salvation, my stronghold. (Ps. 18:2)

> The LORD lives! Praise be to my Rock!
>> Exalted be God My Savior! (Ps. 18:46)

> May these words of my mouth and this meditation of my heart
>> be pleasing in your sight,
>> LORD, my Rock and my Redeemer. (Ps. 19:14)

> For in the day of trouble
>> he will keep me safe in his dwelling;
> he will hide me in the shelter of his tabernacle
>> and set me high upon a rock. (Ps. 27:5)

> In you, LORD, I have taken refuge;
>> let me never be put to shame.
> In your righteousness, rescue me and deliver me;
>> turn your ear to me and save me.
> Be my rock of refuge,
>> to which I can always go;
> give the command to save me,
>> for your are my rock and my fortress. (Ps. 71:1–3)

In the Old Testament, God is portrayed as a large outcropping of limestone rock. He is like the foundation of a mountain, the solid structures sometimes unseen but which keep the entire edifice of life stable. On occasion, "rock" becomes a title as it does in Deuteronomy, "He is the Rock, his works are perfect, and all his ways are just. A faithful God who does no wrong, upright and just is he" (Deut. 32:4). After Saul is defeated, David sings this praise: "The LORD lives! Praise be to my Rock! Exalted be my God, the Rock, my Savior!" (2 Sam. 22:47). And the prophets employ it to call Israel back to its faith in God: "Trust in the LORD forever, for the LORD, the LORD, is the Rock eternal" (Isa. 26:4). This image of God as rock carries two meanings:

BEDROCK INSIDE THE DOME OF THE ROCK

God Is Unchanging

First, we are to learn that God is unchanging. Flashfloods may sweep away homes, wars may desolate entire cities, but the rock, the bedrock of the mountain, will never be changed. God is stable, unchanging, constant, immutable.

When I take friends and students to the Holy Land, I encourage them to examine the rock that has remained for centuries. The Holy Land is filled with historic sites, vistas, and ancient churches. The guarantee of antiquity is found in the carved bedrock—if you know where to look. There are stone steps cut by the Romans on Jerusalem's southern edge, and they still exist today. They were in use during Jesus' lifetime. Some wonder if they were used to take him to Pilate. In Gethsemane we can find more stone steps, used in the first century not far from the site of Jesus' arrest.

The heart of old Jerusalem is the Temple Mount, and at its heart is an outcropping of bedrock over which stands the Muslim Dome of the Rock. Today scholars think that the carvings in this rock stem from the Jewish temple itself, possibly the Most Holy Place. When Jesus traveled to Caesarea Philippi in the north (where Peter gave his remarkable confession that Jesus was the Christ, Mark 8:29), the Roman road crossed a river there; today an ancient Roman bridge still stands, marking where Jesus walked. These are old stones, ancient stones, stones so heavy and well-cut that they have remained for two thousand years.

When the fourth-century pilgrim traveler Egeria (see chap. 1) came to Galilee, she asked to see the steps where "the Lord stood," calling his disciples to shore. They were there in AD 380 for her to see, and they are still there today. In the 1990s I took my daughter to the ancient Church of the Holy Sepulcher where Jesus was buried. She was unimpressed with the ornate accoutrements of centuries of Orthodox and Latin worship. So I took her to the lower levels, deep below Jerusalem's streets, into a cave carved from bedrock, and I told her to place her hands here, on the walls of the stone. "These shook," I said, "when the tomb opened." She liked that.

God's permanence is imaged through the great rocks that form the backbone of this country. They have not changed, nor will they. And they become a potent theological reminder to all who live there.

God and Refuge

Second, God is a refuge as rock is a refuge. Psalm 31:2 says, "Turn your ear to me, come quickly to my rescue; be my rock

Todd Bolen/www.BiblePlaces.com

STEPS AT THE PRIMACY OF PETER

of refuge, a strong fortress to save me." Psalm 71:3 repeats, "Be my rock of refuge, to which I can always go; give the command to save me, for you are my rock and my fortress." This combination of rock and refuge is commonplace, particularly in the psalms, and they refer to something crucial. The wilderness east of Judea is a rocky wilderness, with many excellent places to hide. Erosion has formed many caves; outcroppings of stone give hidden shelters. This explains why David can flee from Saul to the wilderness region of En Gedi for safety (1 Sam. 23:29). There is refuge in the desert mountains.

When corruption seemed to consume Jerusalem's leadership (before Jesus was born), some pious Jews fled to the wilderness near the Dead Sea. On the edge of desert cliffs they built a community apart from the Jewish mainstream that we call Qumran. (We refer to their writings as the Dead Sea Scrolls. In fact, when Roman armies threatened to destroy the community in the first century AD, they hid their scrolls in rock-cut caves deep in the canyons.) Christian monasteries used the desert in the same manner. Mar Saba Monastery east of Bethlehem had caves for dwelling and later thick walls carved from the surrounding mountains.

Safety also came from another source. Since cities like Jerusalem were built on the top of mountains where bedrock was the foundation, cities could be strongholds, anchored to the rock, walled in by solid blocks of stone. Jerusalem evokes that sort of security. On a smaller scale, there was a small Jewish village in northeast Galilee that Jesus knew well. The Jews built it on the top of a mountain, encircled it with stone walls, and defended it against a Roman army. The mountain was shaped

SANDSTONE FORMATIONS IN WHICH CAVE #4 AT QUMRAN IS LOCATED

GAMLA

like a camel hump and so the city was called Gamla (which in Hebrew means "camel").

God therefore can be a place of hiding, a strong place of refuge, a shelter when things go terribly wrong in the wilderness. After Israel left Egypt in the exodus and eventually moved north toward the Holy Land, the terrain changed. Sandy Sinai deserts began to give way to the distinctive terrain of Judea. Rock became a symbol of God. Moses here sang a song of praise, lifting up the "rock-ness" of God:

MAR SABA MONASTERY

> I will proclaim the name of the LORD.
>   Oh, praise the greatness of our God!
> He is the Rock, his works are perfect,
>   and all his ways are just.
> A faithful God who does no wrong,
>   upright and just is he. (Deut. 32:3–4)

Not only will rock represent the great mountain to which God is leading them, but in a partial way, God's provision accompanies them before they arrive. When they travel, a rock appears, the rock of Meribah (Ex. 17:1–7); by striking it, Moses, and with him all of Israel, witnesses a miracle, in that the rock gives water and so provides life.

ROCK AND MEMORIALS

In addition to giving a poignant reminder of God's character, rocks served one more purpose in antiquity. They were reminders. They became "place holders" in history to which people could return in order to revive a memory of what God had done.

Today this tradition continues. If someone visits a Jewish or Muslim cemetery, they will not take along flowers but instead will set a small stone on top of the grave. These stones collect and remain and soon become a monument. On a recent visit to Jerusalem, I read early one morning about a tragedy: an Israeli soldier had been killed during the night on a lane in the Old

ANCIENT JEWISH CEMETERY ON MT. OLIVES, THE OLDEST AND LARGEST JEWISH GRAVEYARD IN THE WORLD.

THE BIBLE AND THE LAND

City near our residence. By morning his body had been removed but blood stains still marked the pavement—and word of the death had spread throughout the city. Quietly Jewish pedestrians rerouted themselves to walk that way, each carrying a small stone. By noon a sizable pile had been built on the site—and it remained there for weeks. A memorial had been erected.

In the wilderness areas tribal regions are still marked with small stone piles (called cairns) that indicate an historic landmark or border. This is simply the continuation of something ancient. A recent field survey in southern Israel found 142 standing stone markers that come from antiquity. Boundaries, histories, memories. Stones mark history.

Biblical Cairns

This idea that stone markers should mark life is a common Old Testament theme. When Samuel defeated the Philistines at Mizpah, he memorialized the victory with a stone cairn called "Ebenezer" (or "stone of help," 1 Sam. 7:12). But the most famous stone marker is recorded in Joshua 4:1–7:

> When the whole nation had finished crossing the Jordan, the LORD said to Joshua, "Choose twelve men from among the people, one from each tribe, and tell them to take up twelve stones from the middle of the Jordan, from right where the priests are standing, and carry them over with you and put them down at the place where you stay tonight."
>
> So Joshua called together the twelve men he had appointed from the Israelites, one from each tribe, and said to them, "Go over before the ark of the LORD your God into the middle of the Jordan. Each of you is to take up a stone on his shoulder, according to the number of the tribes of the Israelites, to serve as a sign among you. In the future, when your children ask you, 'What do these stones mean?' tell them that the flow of the Jordan was cut off before the ark of the covenant of the LORD. When it crossed the Jordan, the waters of the Jordan were cut off. These stones are to be a memorial to the people of Israel forever."

Joshua's instruction is important. In the future, when the memory of the crossing of the Jordan grows dim, Joshua expects that the marker will serve as a reminder for the children of these Israelites. Twelve men take large stones from the river bed, carry them with their first steps into the Holy Land, and pile them carefully to build a cairn, a marker of what has just occurred.

The Logic of the Cairn

These collections of rock hold timeless spiritual lessons. For one, they are a permanent reminder of God's faithfulness in the past. Joshua knows that memory is fickle. And when new struggles come, when new times of confusion, suffering, or dismay erupt, the faithfulness and character of God will be forgotten. The biblical cairn serves as a prompt for memory because we forget the many times God has been faithful. Joshua foresees Israelites bringing their children to this cairn (Josh. 4:6), telling them stories about God's goodness in the wilderness (4:7), and pointing to the stones as physical markers in time and space so that memory will not be lost.

Likewise, one way to keep ourselves from being tossed about by the crisis of the moment is to rehearse the faithfulness of God in the past. One way to keep from being mired in the present is to have a firm grip on the path you've already traveled.

The second value of the biblical cairn is that it puts a present catastrophe in perspective. When the crisis of the moment overwhelms us, we find ourselves consumed by it, obsessed with gaining a way out and doubting whether we will survive. The antidote to the emotional upheavals of the present is to know our history with God, to know where we've already come, to remember the larger obstacle we've already overcome. History has a way of giving us perspective and understanding; without a reminder, without a cairn, we are left with the worries of the present.

ROCK AND FAITH

When students visit my office, they often comment on an odd collection of stones I have in a basket. These stones are my own personal "cairn." Their geological origin is of little interest to me since they serve but one purpose: to give me reminders of what God done for his people—and for me.

First, there are biblical stones. I have a rock from the Elah Valley, where David finished off Goliath (reminding me of God's ability to empower). I have a stone from the bottom of the Sea of Galilee (reminding me of Jesus' miracles there). One stone fell from the ancient palace wall at Babylon, another from Nineveh—both are reminders of how great empires collapse. Another was cut by an ancient chiseler from the side of

VALLEY OF ELAH

Jerusalem's temple, reminding me of God's holy presence in a time and place. There are a lot of these rocks — twenty-five, perhaps — and each tells a story about God's work in history. They come from Egypt, Israel, Palestine, Jordan, and Iraq.

Second, there are other rocks mixed with the first that come from my own personal life. I have a lot of stones from California where I grew up: Riverside, Laguna Beach, and the Merced River in Yosemite Valley. Still others are markers of events that came later in my adult life: I have stones from Pasadena, Aberdeen, Beirut, Damascus, Bristol, Beita, Twin Lakes, Cambridge, and Wheaton. Each of these stones — at least fifteen of them — likewise tells a story. (But it is a private story, as each of our stories must be.)

The principle here is that I need two sets of stones. I need stones that remind me of God's faithfulness in biblical history; and I need stones that remind me of God's faithfulness in my personal history. If I do not work diligently to keep a record of what he has done, my memory of his work fails. And without memory, I am left to the vicissitudes and uncertainties of the present, not trusting that God will be faithful.

"Stones of remembrance" are markers for memory. Without them, I forget. With them, I have a tool that increases my confidence in God's faithful participation in my life.

Chapter 6

WATER

Deuteronomy 11:10; John 4:1–30; 7:37–39

THOSE OF us who live in North America or Europe think little about water. Rainfall averages are generally ample; if anything, we may experience flooding. This is the opposite of life in the Holy Land. This land has always been an arid desert. Leaders of modern archaeological digs must constantly remind volunteers about dehydration. "Time to drink up" can be heard from five-meter dig squares all over the country every summer. I remember the only time I saw a young student fall from heat exhaustion and dehydration. He had refused to wear a hat and would not carry a water bottle; he dropped on the ground somewhere outside New Testament Jericho.

Life in the wilderness makes us preoccupied with water. If we are not, we are foolish. Water keeps us alive, not only refreshing us but also giving something essential for living. Oddly, the wilderness where God sometimes leads us lacks this very thing. God takes us places that do not have the first thing we need to live: water.

THE MODERN STRUGGLE

The people of the Middle East think about water constantly; it is the "oil" of the Holy Land. And if you control it, you have power. Glimpses of this reality are hidden behind many political

THE SEA OF GALILEE FROM THE NORTHWEST

struggles. For example, 8,000 Israeli Gaza settlers once lived among 1.1 million Arabs—but these settlers were sitting on 40 percent of Gaza's water reserves. Syria wants access to its old borders in Galilee (before 1967), but giving this to them means they would have access to the Sea of Galilee—the region's freshwater reservoir—something the Israelis would never permit.

Both Israel and Jordan share access to the Yarmuk River, which has the same volume as the Jordan as it flows through the cliffs southeast of Galilee. Yet both countries watch carefully how much the other pulls from the system. When Arabs grow olives, they have chosen an ancient crop that can live with very little water. When Israelis grow oranges, they produce a crop that requires ten times more water; as Arab politicians say, exporting oranges to Europe is really like exporting water.

The problem, of course, is that the country has limited rainfall and has no centrally located river system. True, the land has the Jordan River, but it is far from the main population centers. The country's central mountains are limestone, which act like a sponge holding a tremendous amount of water in two huge underground aquifers. But this too becomes a political problem. When Israelis use powered drills and modern pumps to pull water from the water table (and forbid their use in Arab villages), they lower the table and suddenly ancient, hand-dug Arab wells go dry. Some Palestinian villages with ancient wells now purchase water from trucks.

THE BIBLICAL WORLD

The biblical world had similar worries about water and its scarcity. When the rains failed to come, when springs dried up and wells went dry, drought and famine became a reality. This was why Abraham migrated to Egypt (Gen. 12:10). Joseph predicted seven years of drought and famine (Gen. 41), which led to his brothers coming to Egypt in desperation "for the famine was in the land of Canaan also" (Gen. 42:5). Naomi and her husband traveled to Moab (present-day Jordan) because of a famine (Ruth 1:1), and David had to weather a three-year drought as well (2 Sam. 21:1). When the Babylonians attacked Jerusalem, they destroyed the region's water systems, which led to a devastating famine (cf. 2 Kings 25:3).

This threat of drought and famine continued through the New Testament era. We have records of ten famines that swept through the Holy Land during the Roman period alone. In Jesus' parable, a drought-induced famine leads the prodigal to return home (Luke 15:14). And later in the church, predictions of famine mobilized Christians to care for one another. Luke reports in Acts 11:28 that a prophet named Agabus "stood up and through the Spirit predicted that a severe famine would spread over the entire Roman world. (This happened during the reign of Claudius.)" Christians in Antioch (who lived along a river) immediately sent aid south to the Christians there (Acts 11:29).

Biblical cultures therefore developed systems to protect them from drought. Cities grew near natural springs. The name of the city of Beersheba refers to

ANCIENT WELL IN ISRAEL

the "seven springs" found there. In Galilee, ancient Tabgha near Capernaum is an abbreviation of the Greek name Heptapagon, meaning "seven springs," named after those found there.

Another solution was to dig wells that could descend into the bedrock and locate the water table. Wells were well known to travelers, and they were covered with a stone for safety (Gen. 29:2). Since these were dug into bedrock, the ancient wells remain today. Scholars chart their number and location in order to estimate the size of ancient settlements and their populations.

In antiquity, gathering water from wells became a woman's occupation. In some respects the well became a place where women could gather to share local news and make plans when, otherwise, their lives were kept in relative isolation. When Abraham worried about how he would find a wife for his son Isaac, he sent his most-trusted servant back to Haran in Mesopotamia with ten camels, hoping the servant would find a woman from his own tribe. Genesis describes the shrewdness of the servant:

> He had the camels kneel down near the well outside the town; it was toward evening, the time the women go out to draw water.
> Then he prayed, "LORD, God of my master Abraham, make me successful today, and show kindness to my master Abraham. See, I am standing beside this spring, and the daughters of the townspeople are coming out to draw water. May it be that when I say to a girl, 'Please let down your jar that I may have a drink,' and she says, 'Drink, and I'll water your camels too'—let her be the one you have chosen for your servant Isaac. By this I will know that you have shown kindness to my master." (Gen. 24:11–14)

The strategy worked, and soon Rebekah was on a camel heading back to Canaan with Abraham's servant. This notion of finding women at wells was commonplace. Jacob met Rachel at a well (Gen. 29:1–14). Moses met his wife Zipporah also at a well (Ex. 2:15–22). The village well was thus the setting for betrothal. As we will see momentarily, this theme is picked up in the Gospels when Jesus arrives at a well in Samaria and there meets a woman who has had a tumultuous marriage history.

The last solution for the problem of drought called for water collection and storage. In this case, communities dug large caverns into the bedrock and lined them with plaster so that they would be watertight. Then winter rains were channeled into the "cistern," a lid covered it (to prevent algae), and the water was held for the year. Today there are cisterns in Israel so large an entire modern building could fit inside. Twelve huge cisterns at the mountain fortress of Masada together held 40,000 cubic meters or about 10.5 million gallons of water.

Elsewhere homes might have had a small private cistern. Today many of these are still in use, and in Palestinian village homes I have been offered a drink of water from the center of a kitchen, where the pitcher came up through the floor on a rope. Cisterns still work.

WATER SYMBOLS AND RITUAL

The seriousness with which biblical culture thought about water should not surprise us. Rainfall determined the fertility of the land and the success of every crop. Since the development of water sources (such as engineering a river) was not humanly possible, it became clear that God alone held Israel's agricultural destiny in hand.

Water was crucial as well in gestures of hospitality in biblical culture. Water for foot washing was the first thing given to a guest before a meal (Gen. 18:4; 24:32). It was also the duty of a house to offer water to strangers who merely passed by (24:17, 43). In fact, to refuse to do this was a gesture of hostility, as when the Israelites passed through Moab and Edom and were refused water even for money.

Water also played a vital role in Israel's religious traditions. Ritual purification viewed water as an essential ingredient for lepers, for sickness, for utensil washing, and for cleansing after touching a dead body (cf. Lev. 15; Num. 5:2). Water was so precious that it was even used as an offering, or libation, before God (1 Sam. 7:5 – 6). At the temple, the forgiveness of sins was symbolized with the ritual sprinkling of water (Ezek. 36:25).

Living Water, Common Water

Qualitative distinctions about water were also common. The rain in autumn brought festival celebrations every October. Hillside springs that rose after the rainy season were further signs of God's blessing. This was compared with water that had been stored in cisterns and held throughout the year. In Jesus' day, Judaism made a careful distinction not in the goodness or taste of water (as though spring water were inherently better), but in its source. Spring water was put to use in Israel's regular religious rituals.

Judaism distinguished between "living" water and common water. In fact, the oral law of early Judaism (the Mishnah) devoted an entire chapter to the classification of types of water for special uses (*Mikva'ot*). Its first section even classifies six grades of water and their religious value! Living water is not a reference to "moving" water or "fresh" water per se. Living water is water that has come to us directly from the hand of God (e.g., rain, a spring, a river). It is water that has not been "ported" or "lifted" by human hand—as stored water has—and so carries a divine potency (Mishnah, *Mikva'ot* 3–4). Of course, such living water is generally free and moving, but that character is secondary to its origin.

Many Jewish purification rituals had to take place in such living water. For instance, at Qumran (where the Dead Sea Scrolls were found) the community believed in regular baptismal washings. These baths (Heb. *mikva'ot*) could not be filled with ordinary *carried* water, but needed a direct link to a spring that flowed from nearby hills. Thus, Qumran today shows an intricate network of channels that moved rain water into the community and distributed it into ritual baths without human

STONE *MIKVEH* OR JEWISH RITUAL BATH

THE BIBLE AND THE LAND

interference. In fact, this living water was considered to be so potent that only a drop of it was required to transform an entire bath of common water into something that would cleanse ritually. Living water had the power to cleanse and purify.

This also helps us understand why John the Baptist required the residents of Jerusalem to hike through the wilderness and come to the Jordan River for baptism. While purifying water could be found in Jerusalem, John claims that they must enter *this living water* to be spiritually cleansed.

Such living water symbolized the life-giving, cleansing work that only comes from God. Among some rabbis, it came to even represent the Holy Spirit. Isaiah makes good use of this imagery to describe what happens when the Lord visits people whose lives are like drought-stricken land:

> For I will pour water on the thirsty land,
>   and streams on the dry ground;
> I will pour out my Spirit on your offspring,
>   and my blessing on your descendants. (Isa. 44:3)

> Come, all you who are thirsty,
>   come to the waters;
> and you who have no money,
>   come, buy and eat!
> Come, buy wine and milk
>   without money and without cost. (Isa. 55:1)

> The LORD will guide you always;
>   he will satisfy your needs in a sun-scorched land
>   and will strengthen your frame.
> You will be like a well-watered garden,
>   like a spring whose waters never fail. (Isa. 58:11)

If living water could cleanse, purify, and bring new life, then God's complete transformation of the world at the end of time would do the same. Zechariah thinks about what will happen when God finally reclaims this world for himself and purifies Jerusalem. He envisions a geyser bursting from the heart of Jerusalem, cleansing it completely: "On that day living water will flow out from Jerusalem, half of it east to the Dead Sea and half of it west to Mediterranean Sea, in summer and in winter" (Zech. 14:8).

SUKKAH (TEMOPRARY SHELTER) CONSTRUCTED DURING THE FEAST OF BOOTHS

Tabernacles

Each autumn, generally in October, Israel celebrated the conclusion of its harvest cycle by bringing to the temple sacrifices from "tree and vine" to thank God for the season that began in the spring. This week-long ceremony was called Tabernacles (Heb., *Succoth*) because while harvesting the orchards of Israel, men would sleep in temporary shelters in the fields. (Succoth is the Hebrew word for a "temporary shelter.") Today orthodox Jewish families celebrate this same festival by building such temporary shelters in their gardens.

But in the autumn, two more elements emerged in Jewish ritual. First, the ancient world was keenly aware of the change of seasons and the so-called dying of the sun, especially since the Festival of Tabernacles was celebrated in conjunction with the autumn equinox. The temple hosted ceremonies recognizing this loss of light and implored God to return it in the spring. Light ceremonies involving rarely-used candelabras were erected in the temple courts and lit at night.

But in addition, October was the end of the dry season. And if the "early rains" did not come, the land could be in jeopardy. Therefore, complex water rituals brought pitchers of water from Jerusalem's Gihon Spring every day, and priests poured the water over the altar, again imploring God to bring rain. On the last day of the feast, the great day, this was done seven times, literally washing the temple altar with water.

Jesus knew these ceremonies. He grew up with them. In John 7 we have a record that he attended the great temple ceremonies during this very time. During the light ceremonies he announced, "I am the light of the world" (John 8:12). And on the last day, the great day of the feast,

> Jesus stood and said in a loud voice, "Let anyone who is thirsty come to me and drink. Whoever believes in me, as Scripture has said, rivers of living water will flow from within them." By this he meant the Spirit, whom those who believed in him were later to receive. Up to that time the Spirit had not been given, since Jesus had not yet been glorified. (John 7:37–39)

Not only is Jesus indicating that he can fulfill what the Festival of Tabernacles prayers seek—water—but he has gone further; he is the source of living water, water that can purify, water that comes from within his own life and transforms others. It is no accident that when Jesus is on the cross in John's Gospel, a soldier pierces him with a spear and water, living water, flows from his side (John 19:34). In John's view, Jesus is the divine source of water that renews and purifies.

ONE WOMAN, ONE WELL

Biblical literature will take the themes of water and drought, famine and plenty, purity and sin, wells and women, and move them together to bring about surprising things. When God is blessing, miraculous rains may occur. Or perhaps water will even pour forth from a rock. When God is punishing, the heavens will close and the land will dry up, as it did in the days of Elijah (1 Kings 17).

John 4 describes Jesus traveling north of Jerusalem into the region of Samaria. This was an ancient area with a heritage that went back to Israel's great patriarchs. When he arrived near Shechem, he came to a well that tradition had credited to Jacob, Abraham's grandson. It was a sacred place with many traditions associated with it.

Because Shechem had no river, women collected water at its historic well. They usually came in the early morning or at dusk to avoid the daily heat. Jesus arrives at noon (John 4:6) and there he meets a woman from a Samaritan village. Her arrival *at noon*—in isolation from the social life of the village women—is a clue to her history. She has had a number of failed relationships (five marriages, 4:18) and now lives with a man to whom she is not married. In a word, her life is a catastrophe.

The exchange between Jesus and the woman has been studied in a number of ways but in most cases, interpretations miss the deepest irony of the story. Motifs pile up on one another here: Jews and Samaritans never talked like this; single men and women would never met like this; and a religious man like Jesus would often have little to do with a "sinner" of this order. Nevertheless, Jesus asks her for a drink of water from the well. The woman engages in some light repartee ("Don't you know that Jews and Samaritans don't talk?!" John 4:9) when Jesus says something remarkable: if she asks, he will give her *living water*.

Jesus is not offering a source of water that is superior to the well (this well is renowned!). He is not suggesting he knows where a river or spring can be found that is more convenient (the woman knows better). He offers her living water (John 4:10) that will become an inner life-giving spring (4:14).

What is this offer? It is not about refreshment, nor is it a gesture to help her with her chore. *It is an offer for her to be cleansed and made new.* Because of her history, this woman probably had not been permitted to come near any Jewish ritual baths of personal purification for years. For instance, women used such ritual baths following each menstrual period, but if she was alienated

JACOB'S WELL INSIDE A CHURCH AT SHECHEM

THE BIBLE AND THE LAND

from her religious community, she lived with an alienating status (called "unclean") and rarely if ever participated in religious life. But now this man, this religious man, this teacher was offering something she could not gain for herself. It was something no one else would give.

The offer of cleansing (and not mere refreshment) explains why Jesus probes the moral history of this woman (John 4:16–19). Renewal and cleansing comes on the other side of repentance. Remarkably, rather than walking away, rather than reviling Jesus' prophetic words (4:19), the woman acknowledges that Jesus is a prophet and, in the end, returns to her village as an evangelist (4:39). A woman whose life has never experienced a man of noble character, whose marriages have all ended in failure, has now stepped accidentally into an ancient betrothal scene—a well—and found true love and forgiveness.

WATER AND FAITH

Biblical culture knew very well that water was essential for life. Too many droughts and famines had swept the land. Too many had died. They prayed for rain annually and recognized that God alone controlled their fate. Each passing dry and rainy season reminded them. Water was valued, it was used in countless cultural rituals, and it came to represent important things. Those of us with water on tap have been disconnected from one of the most powerful reminders of our frailty and our need for God's provision and cleansing.

But the rabbis knew that water was not enough. True life, life at its richest, was not sustained simply with a cistern. Life was not even sustained with a well that came with all of its traditions and history and memories. Water that came directly from God was a deeper symbol of the Holy Spirit, who would refresh, renew, and cleanse better than the ritual synagogue bath used every week. This is why Jesus cannot refer to living water without referring to the Holy Spirit (John 4:23–24; 7:39). God is the only source of true life and in the Holy Land, he formed in his people a keen sense of his life-giving provision, with water that came "directly from his hand."

Chapter 7

BREAD

Exodus 16:1 – 21; John 6:1 – 58

WHEN THE Israelites were in the wilderness, they needed two
things: water and bread. These were the essential elements that
determined their survival. With respect to water, in the great
wilderness story of Israel, God either led his people to sources
of water or supplied it miraculously from rock.

As for bread, there was manna. This was received as "bread
from heaven," giving the people the bare essentials that would
get them through. Without water in the wilderness we become
desperate and fearful almost immediately. But once the oasis is
ours, it doesn't take long before demands for food become shrill.

This is the continuing story of life in the wilderness. It is
indeed a treacherous place, but we do not enter there alone.
Shepherds direct our passage, leading us to water and safety.
And we are fed. In biblical culture (as well as today) bread
becomes an important symbol that reminds us of God's faithful provision. Jesus knows this and in his well-known prayer,
he urges us to say, "Give us today our *daily bread*" (Matt. 6:11,
italics added).

BREAD AND THE LAND

How a culture thinks about its food reveals something about its
history and its traditions. In major metropolitan centers such

WHEATFIELD NEAR GATH
Todd Bolen/www.BiblePlaces.com

as New York, London, or Paris, studying the grocery stores in a neighborhood tells immediately who lives there. In Cambridge, England, one only has to turn down Mill Road to find a number of Pakistani and Indian grocers. Inside are all the characteristic tastes that make up the central Asian diet. In London (as in most British cities), everyone is familiar with Indian "take away" (or "fast food"). The British history in India in the nineteenth century may help explain why. How these cultures employ food tells something about their cultural values and their histories.

Americans eat out frequently at restaurants (often fast food restaurants), and this is yet another signal of cultural values: time and efficiency. A meal in Cairo may take two hours; a meal in Los Angeles, thirty minutes. Egyptians like to eat dinner late at 8:30 p.m. The culture provides a good answer why they do this. The hot climate of Egypt (and other desert Arab cultures) influences them to postpone mealtimes until the cool of the night.

In the West we have lost an awareness of where our food comes from since the modern supermarket offers everything to us in cellophane and cardboard. Our food is also so plentiful that we

IN CAMBRIDGE, ENGLAND, ONE ONLY HAS TO TURN DOWN MILL ROAD TO FIND A NUMBER OF PAKISTANI AND INDIAN GROCERS

likewise have lost any sense of gratitude for it. We have kept ceremonial foods for each season (pumpkin, birthday cake, chocolate Easter bunnies), but we have not retained a daily reminder of the sanctity of the gift of food. Today "hot cross buns" can be found weekly in English bakeries, but who remembers why British law used to limit them to a certain week in spring?

The Modern Context

Both Arabs and Jews hold bread with reverence. I spent an evening once in a Jewish settlement called Beth El. I was visiting the home of a rabbi and at the beginning of the meal, he "broke" the bread and then asked me why it should be wrong to cut bread with a knife. I had no idea. Rabbis everywhere seem to enjoy using public questions for instruction. "Because," he lectured me, "when you cut bread, you do violence to it." My mind wandered to bakeries at home where electric slicing machines made quick work of a loaf. I knew better than to bring it up.

On another occasion I was in the home of Palestinian Christians north of Jerusalem. A woman had decided to teach one of my daughters the art of Arab bread-making. As the bread entered the oven I noticed something odd. With olive oil, she placed a cross on each piece as it left her hands. I asked about it and she was embarrassed. "My mother and grandmother taught me to do this. It's something we do to bless the bread."

In these cultures bread is as much symbol as food. Among Arabs it is a token of hospitality, and long apologies are given if fresh bread cannot be offered to a guest. The Jewish Sabbath service begins with four blessings. The children are blessed, the wine is blessed (the Shabbat Kiddush, or Sabbath blessing), hands are washed (followed by silence), and then with quiet reverence, the bread is blessed: "Blessed are You, Eternal One our God, Ruler of the Universe, who brings forth bread from the earth." Each person breaks off a piece of bread, salts it (as ancient sacrifices were salted), eats, and shouts *Shabbat Shalom*!

Biblical Culture

In antiquity bread made from barley or wheat was the main staple of life. Meat and vegetables were supplements (Gen. 25:34; 27:17; Ruth 2:14). There were no utensils; bread served as spoon and fork. This can be

PASSOVER MEAL

seen in Jesus' final Passover meal in John 13. He identifies his betrayer by offering him something to eat: a piece of bread dipped in a common dish.

The traditional bread of Israel (as it is among Arab Bedouin today) had no yeast and was called "unleavened" (Gen. 19:3; Judg. 6:19, NRSV). This "mazzot" bread is what was used in the Passover meal. When the Bible refers to a "loaf" of bread, the term refers to shape:

SIMILARITY BETWEEN A LOAF OF BREAD AND A ROCK

ancient bread was round (Heb., *kikkar lekhem*, Ex. 29:23). Since the limestone of the wilderness erodes in colors reminiscent of this bread, we can see why Satan showed Jesus wilderness rocks and challenged him to change these into bread; they looked alike (Matt. 4:3). Jesus also told a parable about a son who asks his father for bread; "Will [he] give him a stone?" Of course not! (Matt. 7:9).

Bread was viewed as the primary gift that grew from the earth and sustained life (Job 28:5; Ps. 104:14; Isa. 30:23). At the temple, such gifts were offered as sacrifices. Each Sabbath twelve loaves of bread (baked with frankincense), one for each tribe, were placed on a table and offered to God. This was called "showbread" (ASV)—literally, "bread of the face" (in Heb., *lekhem happanim*) because it was set before "the face of God" (Ex. 25:30; 35:13). The following Sabbath the priests could eat the loaves, but this sacred meal had to take place within the temple.

Bread was more than simply a sacrifice. To break bread meant to have fellowship; thus, sharing bread with God in the temple symbolized divine fellowship. When this "table of showbread" was set, the book of Numbers established directions for the meal: "Over the table of the Presence they are to spread a blue cloth and put on it the plates, dishes and bowls, and the jars for drink offerings" (Num. 4:7). Leviticus 24 even provides a recipe for the bread. All of this evokes images of hospitality, meeting God and sharing fellowship with him.

It is no wonder that in antiquity, threshing floors where grain was sifted from chaff became places of worship. This was the site where God's bounty reached people's need. Grain sacrifices brought to God were thus called "offerings from the threshing floor" (Num. 15:20; 18:27, 30). It is no accident that when David selects a site for God's temple in Jerusalem, he chooses a threshing floor on which to build (2 Sam. 24:18). The public instinctively recognizes it as a conventional site of holiness.

Bread is so basic to life that in Hebrew, it becomes a symbol for all food. In Genesis 3:19, Adam is told that "by the sweat of your brow you will eat your food," but the literal translation is

THRESHING FLOOR

different: Adam will "eat bread." In Psalm 147:9, God provides "food" for both cattle and birds, but here again the Hebrew word is *lekhem* ("bread"). Bread can also be a metaphor: prosperity is described as having "fullness of bread" (Ezek. 16:49, lit. trans. of "overfed"). Charity is "breaking bread" to the hungry (Prov. 22:9). To fast is to "abstain from bread" (2 Sam. 3:35). It is no surprise that in the Hebrew Old Testament *lekhem* is used almost three hundred times.

This wide use is reflected in the New Testament as well. Here the Greek term is *artos*, and like the Hebrew, it is flexible. It can refer to food generally (Matt. 6:11, "give us today our daily bread") or be recognized as the foundation of a meal (Matt. 15:33–36). When Jesus sends out his disciples with "no bread, no bag, no money in your belts," this actually means that they will travel without food, relying on God for their next meal (Mark 6:8).

Of course, the most poignant moment of all comes during Jesus' final Passover meal, when he takes bread used in the course of the meal, turns it into a symbol, and describes it as his own broken body (Mark 14:22). To share this bread with Jesus means fellowship with him *in his death* — the same way as drinking the wine of this meal means participation in his blood poured out (Luke 22:20).

BREAD FROM HEAVEN

Bread invites a cascade of images in the biblical world: fundamental sustenance, sacrifice, fellowship, and hospitality. No meal can be served without bread. No fellowship can be imagined without a meal. To share fellowship with good friends is "to break bread" with them (Acts 2:46; 20:7). To encounter God's presence and provision in some manner likewise involves bread.

The Miracle of Manna

Undoubtedly the most famous bread in the Bible is described in Exodus 16. After Israel fled Egypt, they entered into the wilderness and began their forty-year journey to their Promised Land. After three days, they complained bitterly because they lacked water. God provided an abundance of water at

ELIM

an oasis called Elim (Ex. 15:27). Twelve more days passed
and more complaining echoed throughout the camp: they
had nothing to eat. "If only we had died by the Lord's hand
in Egypt! There we sat around pots of meat and ate all the
food [lit., bread] we wanted" (16:3). Then the Lord makes a
remarkable promise to Moses, "I will rain down bread from
heaven for you" (16:4).

This "bread from heaven" appeared every morning (except
for the Sabbath), and when the people first saw it, they said in
Hebrew, "*Man hu?*" or, "What is it?" This is the origin of our
word "manna." The Israelites asked about this because it was
unusual bread, divine bread, that tapped into every ancient
cultural nuance about bread: it was hospitality, fellowship, and
sustenance. God was welcoming them, feeding them, setting
his table in the wilderness for them.

Three rules followed the descent of "manna." First, manna
gathering was a daily affair. The people could not grow it or
control it. *It was not theirs.* The people could not save it up
(except on the day before Sabbath); every day demanded a fresh
encounter with God's provision—finding and eating divine
bread—which meant reexperiencing his fellowship. Imagine
the effect of this training over forty years.

Second, manna gathering had to be intentional. The manna would melt away by late morning (Ex. 16:21) and therefore gathering it was the priority of each day. At dawn, the Israelites left their tents, gathered what they needed, ate, and then began life. For forty years the early bread ceremony cultivated an instinct to be with God before the day began.

Third, manna gathering was personal. Each family member could collect "one omer" for the day (Ex. 16:16, about two quarts). An enterprising Israelite could not gather up a wagon load of manna and start a distribution business. If someone failed to participate, it was their loss since each could only gather what he or she required for the day.

When Israel later reflected on the most remarkable feats of Moses, rabbis did not consider the opening of the sea, the defeat of Pharaoh's army, or the miracle of water from the rock as Moses' greatest. Instead, the bread miracle of the wilderness that lasted daily for forty years became the signal miracle of his career. In Jesus' day, rabbis explained that in heaven there was a "treasury or storehouse of manna" that opened thanks to Moses' righteousness. And when Joshua led the people across the Jordan River, the treasury closed; the manna stopped descending.

Since this bread miracle was the great miracle of Moses, Judaism looked forward to the day when the treasury would be opened again, when divine bread would feed God's people. As one early Jewish writer put it, "The storehouse of manna shall again descend from on high, and they will eat of it in those years" (2 *Baruch* 29:8).

When would this be? The arrival of the Messiah would provide a "second exodus" for the people. And if this took place, surely the treasury of heaven would reopen. This would be a messianic second exodus in which blessedness would reign down from on high. An early Jewish commentary on Exodus 16:4 says, "As the first redeemer caused manna to descend ... so will the latter redeemer cause manna to descend" (*Midrash Rabbah*, Eccles. 1:9).

Bread, hospitality, and fellowship — they run together to symbolize a deep aspect of Middle Eastern life. Divine bread supplied by God would hallmark the day when God himself would welcome his people.

The Miracle in Galilee

At the height of Jesus' ministry in Galilee, he saw that the crowd had been with him so long that they were without food. He and his disciples discussed their need for "bread," but this should be seen widely as referring to food. They needed a meal. Then, with only five loaves Jesus blessed and distributed the bread, and it was enough (Mark 6:30–44).

The same miracle is told in John 6 but with an important twist. On the following day, people who had observed Jesus multiply the loaves followed him to press him with questions about the bread. They realized that this episode was not about mere bread, nor was it about Jesus' personal generosity. It was Passover season (John 6:4), and the crowds were thinking about the great events of the exodus and Moses' leadership away from Egypt. When the crowd found Jesus, their line of inquiry was precise. Our ancestors witnessed Moses doing this sort of thing — have you reopened the storehouse of manna? Have you duplicated what Moses did (6:25–34)?

Jesus' interpretation of the manna follows rabbinic lines perfectly. First, the true source of the manna was not Moses but God. It is God who sends bread. Furthermore, the manna story goes beyond mere bread — it is a spiritual metaphor for how God feeds us with his word. Deuteronomy 8:3 may well have entered Jesus' debate, "[God] humbled you, causing you to hunger and then feeding you with manna, which neither you nor your ancestors had known, to teach you that people do not live on bread alone but on every word that comes from the mouth of the LORD."

If it is true that God is the source of true heavenly bread — and if it is true that Jesus has been sent by God — the shocking turn in John 6:33 should come as no surprise. The bread of God is a person (he who "comes down from heaven"), a person who "gives life to the world." With a stroke of genius, Jesus has done precisely what he has done throughout his ministry: he has reinterpreted some feature of Jewish belief and ritual so that it would refer to himself.

He is the (symbolic) manna from God's storehouse. He has been sent by God as manna descended in the wilderness. He is the "bread of life" (John 6:35). Therefore — to stretch the image to its outer limits — to eat this bread, to eat Jesus, is to find life (6:57). Why? Because Jesus himself is "bread from heaven"; he is the manna that Israel's ancestors never saw, because eating this bread will not simply sustain life, it will give eternal life (6:58).

BREAD AND FAITH

Jesus' use of bread as a symbol was a constant feature of his teaching. With clear intention, he used it in his final meal — a Passover meal — in order to leave with his followers some sacred ritual that would remain with them after his departure. During this meal he took bread and memorialized it, when broken to represent his own broken body. When consumed, it reflected a participation in his fellowship, a welcoming to his table, a gesture of greeting and unity that he hoped would continue long after his death (Luke 22:19).

If the church has lost sight of the cultural importance of making food sacred, if we no longer view even bread as the gift that it is, we at least need to view this bread, the Eucharistic bread, as a sacred token bearing all of the richness that Jesus intended. For in this bread we claim a reminder — or a reality — of the divine bread offered to us in the descent of God's Son, Jesus Christ.

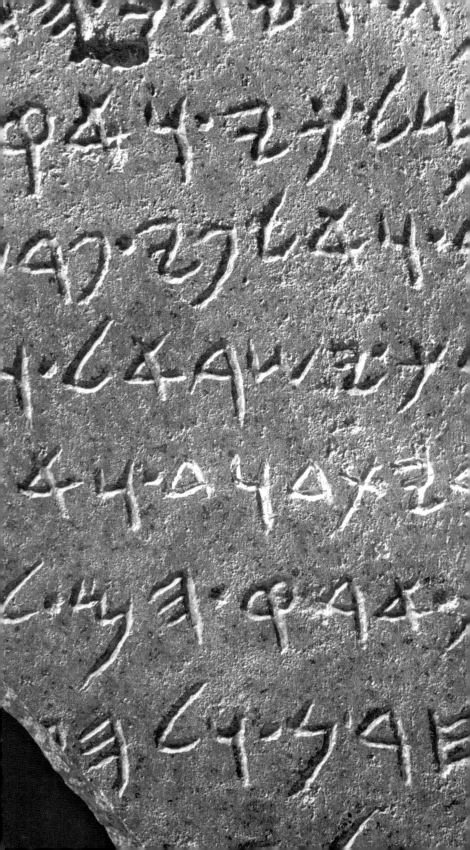

Chapter 8

NAMES

Exodus 3:13–15; Isaiah 43:1–7; Revelation 3:5

THE IDEA of the wilderness is almost synonymous with the idea of loneliness. Jesus apparently rose early in the morning to enter wilderness areas because it was lonely there (Mark 1:35). Another occasion, Jesus took his disciples into a wilderness because of its loneliness (6:31). Once he even used a boat and went to the opposite side of the Sea of Galilee simply to find a lonely respite (Matt. 14:13).

Those who live their lives alongside the wilderness—who enter that wilderness—will always talk about their sense of isolation, their sense of being alone, their wondering whether anyone knows that they are there. The wilderness makes us feel nameless. Its vastness underscores our isolation, and a sense of anonymity settles in with time. *Does God have any idea who I am? Does he have any sympathy with my plight, my desperation, or my fear?* In the wilderness you feel as though you could die and no one would mark your grave, much less find your body.

This opens up another avenue of biblical culture. Not only does God guide us in the wilderness, supplying us with what we need, but he knows us. He understands us more profoundly than we could ever imagine. And all of this is imbedded in antiquity's use of names.

THE HOUSE OF DAVID INSCRIPTION, DAN, GALILEE

SEA OF GALILEE

Todd Bolen/www.BiblePlaces.com

NAMES AND THE LAND

The Western world is casual with its use of names. A couple of years ago I was sitting in a physician's office waiting for my appointment. A young nursing assistant—she certainly was less than twenty years old—emerged from around the corner and announced publicly the name of the next person to see the doctor. On one occasion she called out the name "Andrew." Carefully an elderly couple lifted themselves from their chairs—they had to be in their eighties—and the girl greeted them. Then she said to the man, "Can I call you Andy?"

I thought: *Why isn't she referring to him as "Mr. Smith" or "Sir"?* He could have been her grandfather. What cultural value presumes that no rules apply when young people address seniors? When did we forget that dignity is lost when inappropriate familiarity is taken?

Recently I was in Cairo teaching at a Protestant seminary. As a part of my trip I visited two Egyptian families that my wife and I sponsor through the relief organization Venture International. We drove by taxi to Cairo's poor el-Weily district and there met Rev. Zakaria Abiskairoon, a man twenty years my senior. He was pastor to fifty families, including our sponsor-families. In Arabic priests are called *"Abuna"* ("father"); Protestant pastors are called "*Assis*" ("pastor"). I never once called this pastor Zakaria—he was Assis. We followed him to his church, and then Assis took us to visit our families.

In the world of the Middle East, conversations must always be graced with titles. How we use names signals the relationship we have with its owner. The culture of the Middle East has sustained a value that is inherent in biblical culture: names and their use are deeply important.

But the importance of private names is not lost on us. When our name is used by a telephone-marketing caller, we feel annoyed. When a used car dealer uses our name too many times in conversation, we become uncomfortable. It feels like an invasion of privacy, as an insincere attempt at friendship. When students in my classes want to remain anonymous and sit in the back row, just learning their names (and using them) immediately changes their relationship to me and the class.

Names are powerful and symbolic. They hold an importance that we intuit, but our culture is not supporting the symbolic power of the name. In the U.S. people drive with their names on automobile license plates. Such behavior is precisely opposite of what one would have found in the biblical world.

BIBLICAL CULTURE

The biblical world employed the notion of "naming" in ways now lost. The frequent use of the term *shem* ("name") in the Old Testament (almost nine hundred times) gives some clue to its significance. Rather than say "praise the LORD," the Old Testament will often say "praise the name of the LORD" (Psalm 148:5; Joel 2:26; etc.). Abraham would not "call on the LORD"; he called on "the name of the LORD" (Gen. 12:8). The third commandment warns against taking, not God, but "God's name" in vain (Ex. 20:7). In David's era, many wanted to build a temple, not simply for the Lord, but a temple "for the Name of the LORD" (1 Kings 3:2; 5:3; 2 Chron. 2:1, 4). In the psalms, prayers are not generally directed to the Lord—but rather to "the name of the LORD" (Ps. 116:4, 13, 17).

The key to this phenomenon is that names were *intimately associated* with the person in antiquity. The name referred to the person; it was closely associated with all that was personal and private about that person. To possess someone's name meant that you had access to that person. The name was deeply private since it indicated identity.

Naming Children

Parents in the biblical world sometimes used a custom common to us, naming a child simply because the name suited the parent's whims. Deborah thus means "bee" (Judg. 4:4) and Esther means "myrtle" (or *Hadassah*, Esth. 2:7). Esau means "hairy" and Edom "reddish."

A more remarkable custom among the Hebrews was to select a name that gave some spiritual value to who this child would be in the economy of Israel's life. Judah thus meant "praise" and Zebulun meant "honor." Fully 10 percent of all Hebrew names employed the name of God in some limited form (Heb., *Yahweh*). Jehoshaphat means "Yahweh gives justice" (Hebrew does not use the "J" sound; the "Jeh" prefix stands for the Hebrew "Yah-").

This explains the number of biblical names that begin with the name of God: Jehoahaz, Jehoiachin, Jehoiada, Jehoiakim, Jehonadab, Jehoram, and Jehu. Each conveys some character of God (Jehoram means "Yahweh is exalted"). Sometimes the name of God is attached to the final syllable: Tob*iah* means "Yahweh is good"; Jerem*iah* is like Jehoram, "exalt Yahweh." The modern Israeli name Netanyahu (Benjamin Netanyahu, the Israeli politician) means "gift [*natan*] of God [*yahu*]."

There was thus a conceptual framework that was important to Hebrew naming. Frequently the name bore some historic significance. Or it could be a marker in family history. When Benjamin was born, his father Jacob named him "Ben-yamin" or "son of my right hand." But Jacob's wife Rachel was dying in childbirth and so called her son "Ben-oni" or "son of my sorrow" (Gen. 35:18, 24). The family retained the name Benjamin.

Isaac's name means "laughter" because that is exactly what his parents did when they learned about Abraham and Sarah's upcoming pregnancy (Gen. 17:17; 18:12; 21:3–7). The Hebrew name Mosheh (or Moses) comes from the verb "to draw up" since Moses was "drawn out" of the Nile River (Ex. 2:10). Occasionally the name of a place referred to some event or circumstance. Babel referred to "gate to God" (its literal meaning in Assyrian), since that was the intention of the tower builders (Gen. 11:9).

The Name of God

In antiquity gods were generally known by their activity or by their association with such things as power, weather (thunder), or even fertility. In the Bible, God is the "God *of heaven*" (Gen. 24:3), the "God *of Abraham*" (26:24), or the "God *of Bethel*" (31:13). Non-Israelites might refer to God by way of geography (hills and valleys, 1 Kings 20:28), but Israelites preferred to use descriptors referring to his revealing and saving work (Ps. 79:9, "God of our salvation," NRSV).

The story of the Old Testament is anchored around one pivotal event: the revealing of God's personal name in the book of Exodus (Ex. 3:13–15). The Lord would no longer need to be called *Elohim* ("God") or *Adonai* ("the Lord"), although these names were still in play. After Moses fled from Egypt, he climbed Mount Sinai and there met God in the form of a burning bush (Ex. 3:2). God revealed his plan to use Moses. As courier of God's judgment on Egypt, Moses would bring freedom to his people. But then in this drama of revelation Moses wanted to know who this God was: "Suppose I go to the Israelites and say to them, 'The God of your fathers has sent me to you,' and they will ask me, 'What is his name?' Then what shall I tell them?" (3:13).

Moses likely wanted a name to take back that would reflect the power he needed to accomplish

EGYPTIAN GOD RA

his task. An Egyptian god such as Ra was identified with the sun and he rode his chariot daily across the sky. Above all, Ra was the patron of Pharaoh and had impressive monumental temples that announced his power to the Egyptians.

God's answer to Moses was unexpected. "I AM WHO I AM"—or in Hebrew, *Yahweh* (Ex. 3:14). "This is what you are to say to the Israelites, 'I AM has sent me to you.' " This remarkable name bore none of the usual associations anyone expected. It implied that this God (unlike the Egyptian gods) existed. This name comes from the Hebrew verb "to be" and means that God is alive or active. This is something that God had never done before, not even to Abraham: "I am the LORD [*Yahweh*]. I appeared to Abraham, to Isaac and to Jacob as God Almighty [*El-Shaddai*], but by my name the LORD I did not make myself known to them" (Ex. 6:2–3).

AMULET CONTAINING THE DIVINE NAME "YAHWEH"

The remainder of the story in Exodus 6–20 bears this out: the defeat of Pharaoh and the rescue of Israel from Egypt give proof of his existence and activity. The name alone was a judgment on all other gods, particularly any in the Egyptian pantheon.

In addition to revealing his name and identity, God did something more. He gave himself to Moses by unveiling his private name (*Yahweh*). And in this gesture—this exchange of names with Moses—Yahweh is making an overture for something more: for mutual knowledge, for connection, for relationship. To know this name implies remarkable privilege. Later in Exodus this culminates in the establishment of a *covenant* or permanent bond between God and his people.

The hallmark of being God's people, therefore, meant that knowledge of God's name was held as a unique privilege. In the Old Testament God's people are called "by his name" (2 Chron. 7:14; cf. Isa. 43:7; Amos 9:12). God's people are known as that place where God chooses "to put his Name . . . for his dwelling" (Deut. 12:5; cf. 12:11, 21). Even the high priest's vestments were marked with God's name; he wore a turban with "HOLY TO THE LORD" printed boldly across the front (Ex. 28:36).

Jesus and the Name of God

Since this was the cultural framework of the biblical world, it is not surprising to find these themes in Jesus' life. Luke tells us how the angel Gabriel indicated to Mary precisely what her child's name would be: "Jesus" (1:31). This name is a Greek form of the Hebrew name "Yeshua" or "Yehoshua" — which is a combination of God's name [yeh-] and the word for salvation [hoshea']. This old Hebrew name is commonly translated as Joshua and it means "Yahweh saves."

But Jesus adopts the same attitude toward names and, in particular, toward God's name. He prays in recognition of the holiness of God's name in the Lord's Prayer (Matt. 6:9). Ministry among his followers is carried out in his name (7:22; 18:5, 20). The work of the church is to make disciples "in the name of the Father and of the Son and of the Holy Spirit" (28:19).

Z. Radovan/www.BibleLandPictures.com

THE NAME "JESUS" IN GREEK

John's Gospel gives special attention to this theme. Belief in Jesus' name is a repeated refrain: "Yet to all who did receive him, to those who believed in his name, he gave the right to become children of God" (John 1:12). When Jesus describes prayer as asking "in his name" (14:13; 15:16), we should not see it as a magic formula—as if attaching the name "Jesus" to a prayer gives it new potency. Rather, this refers to prayer as an outgrowth of a relationship with Christ, who owns this name.

The most interesting development in John's Gospel is Jesus' use of some odd grammar. On seven occasions, Jesus identifies himself using "I am." He says, "I am the bread of life" (John 6:35, 51) as well as the light of the world (8:12; 9:5), the sheep gate (10:7, 9), the good shepherd (10:11, 14), the resurrection and the life (11:25), the way, the truth, and the life (14:6), and the true vine (15:1, 5). The secret to this pattern comes clear when we also see that Jesus says "I am" without referring to anything at all. In 8:24 he says, "Unless you belief that 'I am,' you will surely die in your sins" (8:24, lit. trans.). "I am *what?*" we wonder. Or, "before Abraham was born, I am" (8:58). Jesus wants his followers to believe this about him: "I am" (13:19).

What is happening here? Jesus is imitating in Greek the Hebrew name of God. We have seen that the Hebrew name Yahweh meant "I am." So Jesus is employing this sacred Hebrew name. In John 18:5 – 6 something similar happens. When Jesus identifies himself to his enemies, he again says the holy name (lit., "I am") and immediately his captors fall down. Theirs is an appropriate response to a name so sacred.

EXCHANGING NAMES

These concepts converge into one fundamental idea: God and his people have exchanged names. When this happens, a relationship emerges. In some cases, God supplies the name for a person (such as Adam, Gen. 5:2; or Isaac, 17:19). In some cases God changes the name of one of his people. Abram ("glorious father") becomes Abraham ("father of many"). Sarai becomes Sarah, Jacob becomes Israel, and even Jesus takes this privilege with Simon, who now is called Peter. Jesus even names James and John "sons of thunder" (Mark 3:17). All of this shows an intimate coownership of name and life. Jesus and James now have a unity, a connection that sets their relationship apart. They "know" each other's names.

This interactivity surrounding names means that God knows the names of his people (as we know his name), and he keeps them near to his heart. Typical is Exodus 33:12, where the Lord reassures Moses, "I know you by name and you have found favor with me." When God calls Samuel to be a prophet, he likewise calls him by his name because he knows him personally (1 Sam. 3:1–10). Isaiah says the same for all of God's people:

> But now, this is what the LORD says —
>   he who created you, Jacob,
>   he who formed you, Israel:
> "Do not fear, for I have redeemed you;
>   I have summoned you by name; you are mine." (Isa. 43:1)

The notion of knowing the name is an ancient idiom for something remarkable. The Bible never thinks about us without considering our personal identity before God. When Jesus called Saul on the road to Damascus, imagine his surprise when he heard "Saul, Saul" thundering from heaven. This was no abstract revelation; this was highly personal. Jesus knew his name. In the book of Revelation we read six times about a "book of life" where the names of Jesus' followers are recorded (Rev. 3:5; 17:8; 20:12, 15; 21:27). This is a splendid divine metaphor: Who we are is known at the very center of God's life — and it will not be forgotten. Moreover, Revelation 2;17 tells us that "'those who are victorious," that is, those who persevere in their faithfulness, will be given "a new name written on [a white stone], known only to the one who receives it." It will be an intimate name shared only between us and God. Few images of the wonder of our salvation could be more profound.

The result of this can be transforming. Our faith is not about abstraction; it is about intimacy. It is about a person who in the Old Testament delivered his gospel with the words embedded in ancient idiom: "I have summoned you by name; you are mine" (Isa. 43:1). In the New Testament that same divine overture — that same gospel that comes to be known, reaching to redeem — is found in the coming of Jesus Christ.

In John's Gospel Jesus expressed it well, "I am the good shepherd; I know my sheep and my sheep know me—just as the Father knows me and I know the Father—and I lay down my life for the sheep" (John 10:14–15). This is a revelation! The knowledge shared between Father and Son here becomes the knowledge shared between the good shepherd and his sheep.

THE TRANSFORMING NAME

For a number of years I served as a chaplain in the U.S. Navy. The Navy has a tradition of attaching titles to people and using them as a person's sole identity. I was often called "lieutenant." On ship, I might be called "chaps." The navigation officer was called "Nav." The Operations Officer "Ops." The executive officer was "XO." Of course we had other names, but these were the names we used.

Enlisted personnel often went by their last names, rank ("senior" for "senior chief"), or specialization. An Air Traffic Controller who was a second class petty officer was called AC2. A Religious Programmer, petty officer

Soldier's uniform

mer, petty officer first class (a chaplain's assistant), was known as RP1. We never used their names. We simply asked "RP1" to report to the chapel.

For some time one of my jobs was meeting with discouraged recruits who were at Great Lakes Naval Training Center, the Navy's boot-camp in Chicago. Once I recall meeting with one of the boot camp leaders. His full name was "Fire Control Technician third class MacMillan" (I've changed his name). He was about nineteen or twenty. "FT3" was like so many other young men who had joined the military fleeing a terrible family. He had problems with debt, fighting, and simply following orders. His life was unraveling. FT3's debt came from sending most of his paycheck home every month. His father said he owed it.

Gary M. Burge

Then the story of years of violent childhood abuse emerged. He had been physically abused by a drunken father so many times he couldn't count the episodes. And the man had convinced FT3 that the boy was lucky he was alive—and that he owed his father for bringing him into the world. FT3 bought it. I asked him what the most painful moment was and he told me how the family had planned a trip to Disneyland when he was about fourteen. But he had to save his lawn-mowing money to get himself in. At the gate, he was short about ten dollars. And his father made him sit in the car the entire day while his family went inside and played. It is rare to see a man like this break down. FT3 cried as he described his memories in the parking lot.

I held his file on my lap and remember skimming through his military record as we spoke. And impulsively, breaking protocol, I said, "*Gregory*, you have really suffered."

He looked shocked. "When was the last time you heard your first name here on base?" I asked.

"Eleven months ago."

"When did an officer ever say it?"

"Never."

"Gregory, my name is Gary—and we need to become friends."

If it is possible to express the gospel in unexpected terms, this was it. To be known, to have the sanctity of our name embraced, opens the way to being loved. When this happens, the possibilities for redemption, for hope, and for healing suddenly appear.

NAMES, THE WILDERNESS, AND FAITH

Life lived alongside the wilderness or within the wilderness does not need to be lived alone. Not only does God guide us (as a shepherd), but he knows us. Jesus describes himself as the good shepherd who knows his sheep (Jn 10:14) and delights in calling them by name (John 10:3). And it is within this intimacy of sharing names, of knowing each other, that he becomes their leader in desolate places. The sheep follow because they know this voice and they can trust it. This is the meaning of faith.

Ancient Context, Ancient Faith
Jesus, the Middle Eastern Storyteller

Gary M. Burge

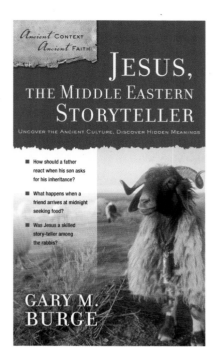

   As the early church moved away from the original cultural setting of the Bible and found its home in the west, Christians lost touch with the ancient world of the Bible. Cultural habits, the particulars of landscape, even the biblical languages soon were unknown. And the cost was enormous: Christians began reading the Bible as foreigners and missing the original images and ideas that shaped a biblical worldview.

   Jesus, the Middle Eastern Storyteller, by New Testament scholar Gary M. Burge, explains that Jesus lived in a story-telling culture that was completely unlike the modern world. When we imagine Jesus' teaching in his own time and place, we cannot use profiles of teachers from our own setting to understand the nature of his work. Jesus' world was different. Burge explains the parables as they have been rarely explained before. He brings new insight to Jesus' view of God and his understanding of the life of discipleship.

   Each volume in the *Ancient Context, Ancient Faith* series is full color, rich with photographs, and in a travel size for convenient Bible study anywhere you go.

Softcover: 978-0-310-28045-3

Share Your Thoughts

With the Author: Your comments will be forwarded to the author when you send them to *zauthor@zondervan.com*.

With Zondervan: Submit your review of this book by writing to *zreview@zondervan.com*.

Free Online Resources at
www.zondervan.com

Zondervan AuthorTracker: Be notified whenever your favorite authors publish new books, go on tour, or post an update about what's happening in their lives.

Daily Bible Verses and Devotions: Enrich your life with daily Bible verses or devotions that help you start every morning focused on God.

Free Email Publications: Sign up for newsletters on fiction, Christian living, church ministry, parenting, and more.

Zondervan Bible Search: Find and compare Bible passages in a variety of translations at www.zondervanbiblesearch.com.

Other Benefits: Register yourself to receive online benefits like coupons and special offers, or to participate in research.

ZONDERVAN®
.com